LESLIE FEINBERG

Rainbow Solidarity
in Defense of
CUBA

lavender
&
red

This book is an edited compilation of chapters
86 to 110 from the Lavender & Red series
in Workers World newspaper

World View Forum
55 West 17 Street, Fifth Floor
New York, NY 10011
June 2009

212-463-7146

Rainbow Solidarity
Library of Congress Control Number: 2008929962

ISBN is: 9780895671509

Front cover photo: May Day celebration in Havana, 1995
Cover photo: Barbara Smith
Cover design: Lal Roohk

Fonts: Adobe Jenson Pro and Myriad Pro

G. Dunkel

THE LAVENDER & RED
SERIES IS DEDICATED TO
PAT CHIN
WHO LIVES IN THE HEARTS
OF HER COMRADES

'Emancipate yourselves
from mental slavery:
None but ourselves
can free our minds'
—Bob Marley

CONTENTS

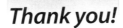

Thank you!

A revolutionary grassroots organizer knows in hir political bones that unity is essential to winning demands—bread-and-butter or life-and-death. Effective political thought and action is by its very nature social, a product of the labor of many. Respect for the power of collective work keeps activists "right sized."

As the communist worker who volunteered to research these articles, document the facts and write them up, I had a lot of help.

First and foremost, this book would not have been possible without the political leadership of Teresa Gutierrez—co-founder of the National Committee to Free the Cuban Five and founder of the New York Committee to Free the Cuban Five.

Lal Roohk brought this text to visual bloom. Soon, with more help, these articles will also be recorded as audio podcasts at www.workers.org.

Lavender & Red editors LeiLani Dowell and Deirdre Griswold paid meticulous political attention to this series of articles. Rebeca Toledo, Shelley Ettinger and Bob McCubbin—all long-time members of Workers World Party's Lesbian/Gay/Bi/Trans Caucus—contributed their acumen as political readers. Bob McCubbin and Minnie Bruce Pratt carefully copyedited. Monica Moorehead, Naomi Cohen, Fred Goldstein, Gary Wilson, Lal Roohk and John Catalinotto added insight to particular articles in this compilation. My appreciation to Sara Flounders for organizational support from start to finish, and to Kathy Durkin for her fund-raising labor. Thanks to Janet Mayes for creating the index.

I thank those who sustained this series with facts and feedback, political discussion and organization, including: Sharon Ayling, Sara Catalinotto, Sue Davis, Julius Dykes, Sharon Eolis, Marsha Goldberg, Sue Harris, Imani Henry, Beverly Hiestand, Berta Joubert-Ceci, Larry Holmes, Michael Kramer, Cheryl LaBash, Dustin Langley, Marge Maloney, Milt Neidenberg, Rosemary Neidenberg, Frank Neisser, Andre Powell, Arturo J. Pérez Saad, Gerry Scoppettuolo and Maggie Vascassenno.

I acknowledge the volunteer labor of all those who work together to produce a revolutionary newspaper, which has published for close to half a century in the U.S., including: late-night proofreaders, and those who study the postal regulations, address and mail the papers, post the current issue on the web, and drop off bundles at coffee shops and delis.

A special thanks to *Workers World* newspaper readers who sent questions and eloquent messages about the impact of the Lavender & Red series on their political outlook.

I owe a historical debt of gratitude to Sam Marcy, founder of Workers World Party in 1959, and party leader Dorothy "Dotty" Ballan.

As a Marxist who analyzed and wrote in the heat of the struggle, Marcy made a historic contribution by building a revolutionary communist organization that understands the need to fight anti-gay and anti-trans oppression.

Dorothy Ballan shaped generations of communist understanding that the fight against women's and sexual oppression is an important front in revolutionary struggle. Ballan broke the system of repressive labor grades for women workers at Westinghouse in Cheektowaga, in upstate New York. As a result, she became the first woman to operate a punch press in the entire history of the U.S. electrical industry.

Lavender & Red series segments 78-85 at www.workers.org look more closely at how Marcy and Ballan helped develop discussion and education inside Workers World Party.

Taken together, all those I've named—and many others to whom I still owe a hand shake—are from many nationalities, who speak different mother tongues; some born in countries around the globe; some born in the U.S. Their ages represent a span of more than half a century. They represent spectra of sexualities, gender expressions and sexes.

This wide-angle snapshot of those who worked together to bring this book to your hands already tells you a lot about Workers World Party.

Warm thanks to Barbara Smith—long-time, respected Black lesbian feminist activist and author—for contributing the powerful cover photo, which she took at a May Day communist celebration in Havana in 1995. Thank you also to each of the photographers who donated their images to this book, including G. Dunkel, Margaret "Peggy" Gilpin, Liz Green, Teresa Gutierrez, Walter Lippmann, Sonja de Vries and Roberto J. Mercado; and to Yamila Azize-Vargas for contributing from her own personal collection a key historical photograph of Luisa Capetillo.

Last, but not at all least, deep gratitude to those who contributed their labor in another form—donations from their weekly wages and fixed incomes and savings—to print and collate and bind and distribute this book as a weapon of fact wielded against mega-monopoly media propaganda. They are:

Supporters: Susan Elizabeth Davis, in loving memory of Bill Haislip and Marshall Yates; Lal Roohk; Gary Schaefer; Charles Twist; Gary Wilson.

Donors: Gray Anderson; Mike Eilenfeldt; Sara Flounders; Mike Gimbel; Deirdre Griswold, in memory of comrade Henri Nereaux; Andre Powell, in memory of William Mena and companero Raoul; Minnie Bruce Pratt; Bill Sacks, Katy Rosen, Emma Sacks, and Malcolm Sacks; Joe Yuskaitis.

Friends: Sharon Ayling, in memory of Bill Haislip; Sharon Black; George Bollag; Lee Booth; Philip Booth; Lillian Carney; Joyce Chediac and Paul Wilcox, in memory of John Crofford; Meg Barden Cline; Naomi Cohen, Lila Goldstein, and Fred Goldstein, in memory of Rachel Nasca; Heather Cottin; Lawrence Daley; Dave Davis; Angel Do-brow; Bob Dobrow; Sharon Eolis, in loving memory of Dorothy Ballan; Irving Fier-stein; Sherry Finkelman; Peter Fiorentino; F.I.S.T. (Fight Imperialism, Stand Together); Mike Gill; Marsha Goldberg and Caro Torrez; Martha Grevatt and Dian Killian; Larry Hales; Jesse Lokahi Heiwa; Imani Henry; Beverly Hiestand; International Action Cen-ter, San Diego; Nina Howes; Sue Kelly; Kathryn Kent; Larry Klein; Linden P. Mar-tineau; Janet Mayes, in memory of Ellen Andors; Bob McAllister; Bob McCubbin, in memory of Ronnie Burk; Jeanette Merrill, in memory of Ed Merrill; Rosario Morales and Dick Levins, in memory of Rachel Nasca; Jim Morgan; Anya Mukarji-Connolly; Reza Namdar; Lyn Neeley; Milt Neidenberg; Rosemary Neidenberg; Frank Neisser, in loving memory of Richard Newkirk; Susan Rotgard; Gloria Rubac, Houston Workers World and Houston Cuba Solidarity Committee; Ariel Ruiz; Brenda Sandburg; Su-san Schnur and Sharon Danann; Gerry Scoppettuolo; Carrie Singleton, in memory of Louise Merrill; Deirdre Sinnott; Harry Staley; Helen Staley; Allen Strasburger; Jim Wallace; Benjamin Weaver; Martha Weisman and Bill Hagel; Women's Fightback Net-work/Boston, in loving memory of Rachel Nasca.

And Workers World branches from Atlanta, in memory of Jim Harlow; Baltimore; Boston; Buffalo; Chicago; Cleveland; Denver; Detroit; Houston; Los Angeles; Philadel-phia, in memory of comrade William Mena; San Diego; San Francisco, in memory of Louise Merrill; and Washington, D.C.

INTRODUCTION

"Rainbow Solidarity in Defense of Cuba" is a compilation of 25 articles about same-sex love and sex/gender variance in Cuba's pre- and post-revolutionary history. These articles make up parts 86 to 110 of the Lavender & Red series, which has run as a feature in *Workers World* weekly newspaper since the first article appeared in the June 3, 2004, issue.

The table of contents for 120 segments of the ongoing series appears in the back of this book. The entire Lavender & Red series is posted for reading on the web: www.workers.org.

Lavender & Red gathers information about the relationship between the struggle for liberation from oppression based on sexuality, gender expression and sex, and the revolutionary movement for socialism, and ultimately for its highest and most humane stage, communism.

Lavender & Red confronts the political view, whether voiced because of demagoguery, demoralization or lack of information, that life under capitalism may be a hard road for lesbian, gay and bisexual, transgender and transsexual people—but socialism is inherently worse. The series offers information about little-known remarkable achievements in the Soviet Union and East Germany and carefully analyzes problems in these workers' states, as well—both of which bolster modern revolutionary theory and practice.

This ongoing historical materialist series answers those who maintain that Marxism as a science either is, or should be, concerned only with the direct struggle between finance capital and the working class. The series argues that class unity can only be cemented by revolutionary solidarity in the struggle against many forms of oppression.

Marx and his comrade Frederick Engels wrote and organized to build support for liberation struggles of oppressed peoples against slavery and colonialism. And Engels wrote an early examination of the roots of women's oppression in the rise of private property, which led to the overturning of communal, pre-class societies and the reorganizing of social, gendered and sexual relations to fit a new world order ruled by the patriarchy.

Lavender & Red indicts class society—slavery, colonialism, capitalism and imperialism—for the ideology of divide and conquer, including racism and anti-homosexual prejudice.

'Gendering' domination

In 1898, North American capitalism burst its boundaries and outfought its colonialist predecessors to claim Cuba, the Philippines and Puerto Rico as U.S. possessions. Imperialist spin doctors developed racist campaigns as ideological cover for invasion, or more covert forms of "regime change." These white supremacist campaigns that spewed claims of racial and moral superiority—stimulants for the reactionary nationalism of an oppressor nation—aimed at dehumanizing peoples who were in the gunsights of U.S. finance capital.

Speaking as the rising voice of imperialist military aggression at the turn of the 20th century, Theodore Roosevelt—who extolled male "virility"—added: "The greatest danger that a long period of profound peace offers to a nation is that of effeminate tendencies in young men." Aggression by the rich, and later the super-rich, whether economic or meted out on their behalf by the armed bodies of the state, has always been "gendered" as masculine, superior and invincible.

An infamous article in the Philadelphia *Manufacturer* on March 6, 1889, was headlined "Do We Want Cuba?" Like Nazi eugenicists, the article—written by several powerful Republican politicians—bandied about the pros and cons of annexing Cuba, referring to Cubans as an "effeminate" people, lacking "virile" strength. (Bejel)

With the imperialist takeover of Cuba came a brutal re-structuring of the division of labor based on the sexes, kinship, family, marriage, sexuality, living accommodations and other aspects of social organization. The drive behind the changes was the insatiable appetite for profits of the banks and corporations. U.S. big business, including crime syndicates, organized urban Cuba into a giant brothel, super-exploiting the sexual labor of Cuban females and males, feminine and masculine, homosexual and heterosexual.

Then came the 1959 revolution. New ways had to be found to criticize and disparage the Cuban people. It became fashionable in imperialist culture to accuse Cuban males of "machismo" of being too "too masculine" When Cubans use the term, they are referring to the legacy of male chauvinism and sex/gender and sexual prejudices inherited from centuries of patriarchal rule by colonialism and imperialism. But in the imperialist oppressor country, the term is chauvinist, blaming Cuban male gender expression for all the ills of patriarchy.

The charge of "hyper masculinity" against men of African descent has been a cornerstone of Jim Crow lynch law within the U.S., as well.

'New man,' 'new woman'

People "make their own history," Karl Marx wrote, "but they do not make it just as they please; they do not make it under circumstances chosen by themselves, but under circumstances directly encountered, given and transmitted from the past."

Since the victory over the U.S.-backed Batista dictatorship in 1959, Cuba has mobilized the people to reorganize the economy to meet the needs of the whole laboring population. As the Cubans say, "It's not easy." It's especially hard when U.S. imperialism is waging covert war and threatening overt war against Cuba, trying to sabotage revolutionary construction at every turn.

Yet this small island nation of 11 million has, for half a century, done what the richest imperialist country on the planet won't do and can't do: provide everyone jobs, food and clothing, a home, free education—from kindergarten to graduate school—and free quality health care, including preventive medicine. The Cuban Revolution has made enormous strides in eliminating racism, which itself required dismantling the apartheid economic and social structures.

The Cuban Revolution elevated mass popular discussion about how to raise a "new man" and a "new woman" in a society still trying to shed the burdens of almost half a millennium of patriarchal class rule and church dogma.

The revolution ushered in sex education and reproductive rights. Revolutionary Cuba is also making qualitative leaps in understanding gender expression.

U.S. airport bookstores are lined with pop psychology publications that claim women and men are from different planets. Cuba's mass discussion about the "new man" and the "new woman," which examines new ways to interact, is light-years ahead ideologically. The whole premise of the island-wide education, discussion and debates is that prejudicial and harmful attitudes and actions resulted from old, oppressive economic and social organization—and not vice-versa.

The mass discussion starts from the understanding that with changed economic and social organization, human beings can change their attitudes, rather than being biologically wired to be oppressive, violent, avaricious or cruel.

Break the U.S. blockade

Of course, there were and are problems in Cuba. That's what half a millennium of colonialism and imperialism leaves—problems. But the problems that exist in Cuba—or any other workers' state—do not invalidate the revolution. Quite the contrary. The process of solving those problems is the forward motion of the revolution.

A lot of facts are assembled between the covers of this book. The facts articulate Cuba's achievements—quantitative gains, as well as qualitative advancements—of which there are many.

These compiled articles are not dispassionate journalism. Political analysts, like historians, always write from a class point of view. But these articles are factually based and are placed where they belong—within the context of a life-and-death struggle to defend Cuba.

You will find no condemnation of the Cuban Revolution in this book. The history of the Cuban Revolution is a process from which we who have not yet made our revolutions have a great deal to learn about the struggle for sexual liberation, based on concrete historical conditions.

Viewed together, the facts in these 25 articles demonstrate Cuba's inexorable progress on social issues, despite the U.S.-enforced economic blockade and unrelenting imperialist covert and overt warfare that drains the country's labor, time, planning, organization and resources for defense.

We hope that, because this material is here amassed in one place for the first time, the reader will be able to get a panoramic view of the forward motion of the Cuban Revolution in the struggle to eradicate the legacy of pre-Revolutionary prejudices against homosexuality, diversity of gender expression, sex variance and sex change.

—Leslie Feinberg
Managing editor,
Workers World newspaper

In June 2007, as this book was first being readied for production, Cuban revolutionary leader Vilma Espín died. The Editorial Board of WW newspaper extends its deepest solidarity at this painful loss for the Cuban people. Espín helped lead the Cuban women's "revolution within the revolution" that has blazed new trails for liberation of sexuality, gender expression and the sexes. She leaves the value of her lifetime of laboring for change to the Cuban people, the Cuban Revolution and the communist movement worldwide.

1970s Cold War
gay-bashers condemn Cuba

Bob McCubbin, a young gay male leader in Workers World Party during the rise of the early gay liberation movement, recalls, "By having regular articles in *Workers World*, attending gay protests, producing and distributing flyers addressing lesbian and gay issues, giving extra visibility to gay comrades, organizing branch meetings on related issues, and doing outreach to the lesbian and gay communities, we were successful in attracting many lesbian and gay youth to our ranks in the early and middle 1970s.

"But this work was not without difficulties," McCubbin says. He remembers, in particular, how a stream of articles in the big-business media opened up a campaign against Cuba. Many of the articles focused on the imperialist charge that gay and lesbian Cubans were being mistreated on the island after the 1959 revolution.

The reality is that the Cuban Revolution—which seized state power on an island in which class society, colonialism and imperialism had woven prejudices and repression against same-sex love tightly into the fabric of life—has made tremendous advances for men who love men and women who love women, as well as the struggle against racism and sexism.

The U.S.-led blockade is designed not only to economically strangle the Cuban population, but to obscure from lesbians, gays, bisexuals and trans people living in the imperialist citadel an understanding about what a revolution can achieve in terms of social progress.

It is impossible to skip over the staggering hypocrisy of U.S. imperialism and its media propaganda machinery. They don't care a whit about lesbian and gay, bisexual and trans lives. They want to crush the revolution and re-enslave the entire population.

Their political duplicity was obvious on the domestic front. In the 1950s, these Cold War capitalists had escalated a state witch hunt against every expression of homosexuality and gender variance under the guise of a "Lavender Scare."

Same-sex love was still illegal across the United States. Gay men, lesbians and all gender-variant people faced police raids and entrapment, prison, torture, forced institutionalization, rape and lynchings, loss of jobs, homes and loved ones. (See Lavender & Red series, parts 26-28, www.workers.org.)

But by the 1970s—while cops were still raiding bars after Stonewall and same-sex love was still illegal—the imperialists suddenly became champions of gay rights, anywhere except on their own soil.

The big-business spin made it seem as though the Cuban Revolution was a wellspring of anti-gay prejudice.

"Absent the persistent and pervasive climate of anti-communism," McCubbin stresses, "such attacks would have been laughable, emanating as they did from a country where gay-baiting was an indispensable political tool and where scarcely a week went by without the murder, somewhere within the U.S., of a transgender person.

"But since the anti-Cuba propaganda campaign was relentless and did have a negative effect on many people, including many lesbian and gay youth, we felt a serious responsibility to answer and challenge these articles, and we did, just as we conscientiously defended the other socialist countries, and in particular the Soviet Union, from the steady stream of anti-communist attacks.

"So we were often challenged by progressive youth, gay and straight: 'You support Cuba?' The more serious listened carefully to what we had to say in Cuba's defense, but we were also badmouthed frequently by anti-communist elements in the gay movement."

Understanding the Cuban Revolution, and the hand it was dealt by imperialism, is as important today as it was then, because it demonstrates what a revolution can achieve, even when surrounded and under siege by imperialism.

The truth to begin with is this: Communists did not bring anti-homosexual prejudice to the Americas. The development of class societies and colonialism did. ▼

Colonialism: the real 'Apocalypto'

From Indigenous oral histories, passed down through millennia, to the hostile accounts kept by colonial record keepers, a great deal of evidence exists to show that sex/gender variance and homosexuality were part of the fabric of early cooperative societies in the Americas—from pole to pole.

What is significant about the abundant European colonial records—whether military, missionary or anthropological—is not their perceptivity, objectivity or accuracy in describing life among the diverse Native societies in this hemisphere. It's that these observations by the Europeans and their reactions to homosexuality and gender/sex variance in Native cultures—reflected in characterizations like "devilish," "sinful," "perverted," "abominable," "unnatural," "heinous," "disgusting," "lewd"—reveal how different the European societies were.

The "observed" were peoples who lived in societies that were either communal or were in the early stages of class division.

The "observers" came as military, commercial or intellectual servants of entrenched European ruling classes that were expanding beyond their own hemisphere to steal gold, land and other resources.

In Europe, where most communal lands had been seized by slave-owners and then feudal landlords, state laws and repression against same-sex love and sex/gender variance had been part of this centuries-old class warfare.

From south to north

Colonial observations about same-sex love and sex/gender variance in Indigenous societies in the Western hemisphere are copious. Those with imperial aspirations studied the peoples they sought to militarily conquer and enslave.

When a European colonial expedition in 1576 reached the lands of the Tupinamba people in what is now northeastern Brazil, they found female-bodied hunters and warriors who were accepted by the other Native men. Recalling the Greek Amazon warriors, the Europeans dubbed the river that flowed through that area the "River of the Amazons." (Magalhães)

Narrating his first trip down another river, now called the Mississippi, Jesuit Jacques Marquette described in the 17th century how, among the Illinois and Nadouessi, he found people who today would be referred to as Two-Spirit. Marquette wrote that they were "summoned to the Councils, and nothing can be decided without their advice. Finally, through their profession of Leading an Extraordinary life, they pass for Manitous— That is to say, for Spirits—or persons of Consequence." (Marquette)

French missionary Joseph François Lafitau condemned the Two-Spirit people he found in societies along the western Great Lakes, Louisiana and Florida, but these Native peoples did not share his prejudice. He wrote in 1724 that "they participate in all religious ceremonies, and this profession of an extraordinary life causes them to be regarded as people of a higher order." (Lafitau)

But where Indigenous ruling classes had emerged and consolidated their territory, sometimes after the violent overturn of neighboring communal societies, these attitudes had changed.

Historian Max Mejía wrote, "In the Aztec culture of pre-Hispanic Mexico, the dominant culture at the time the Spanish arrived, the treatment of sodomy was not exactly favorable. On the contrary, the Aztecs had very harsh laws against it, punishing the practice severely with public execution for those who were caught. Punishment affected mainly males, but women were not exempt." (Mejía)

Friar Bartolomé de las Casas noted that among the Aztecs, "The man who dressed as a woman, or the woman found dressed with men's clothes, died because of this."

"However," Mejía explained, "there were exceptions to the Aztecs' rules against homosexuality. Most historians agree that the practice was tolerated when it took place in religious rituals."

Mejía added, "[T]he Aztecs ruled over a vast array of peoples, who had different cultural histories. Several of these did not necessarily share the Aztecs' vision of homosexuality and its practice. Some even showed signs of singular tolerance towards it in their communities. One of these was the Zapotec culture, derived from the Mayans and located in what is now the state of Oaxaca."

He emphasized, "[W]hat I am trying to show is that in pre-Hispanic Mexico, alongside the rigid Aztecs, there existed—and there exist still today—other, more flexible cultures more tolerant of homosexuality."

When it came to sexuality, Mejía stated: "[T]he Mayans had a more favorable view of diversity within the community, which suggests greater tolerance of homosexuality, above all when it concerned religious rituals and artistic practices."

The real "Apocalypto"

In 2006, director Mel Gibson made a movie called "Apocalypto" about the Mayan empire, as experienced by a family from a nearby hunting-gathering society being chased by its warriors.

Gibson's movie ideologically serves those in the U.S. who yearn for a Fourth Reich, much as Leni Riefenstahl's films did for imperialist Nazi capital.

"Apocalypto," which depicts the Mayans as inherently bloodthirsty, is being screened in the citadel of the most bloodthirsty imperialist power in history. It arrives in chain

Valboa Indos nefandum Sodomiæ fcelus com- **XXII.**
mittentes, canibus objicit dilaniandos.

ALBOA in ista ad montes profectione Regulum in Efquaragua fuperat & cædit cum multis Indis: pagum deinde ingreffus Reguli fratrem & alios quofdam muliebri veftitu ornatos: valde admiratus, caufam fcifcitatur: intelligit cæfum Regulum & omnes eius aulicos nefando illo peccato naturæ aduerfo infectos. Attonitus Valboa adeo deteftabile fcelus ad iftos Barbaros penetraffe, corripi omnes iubet numero forte quadraginta, & canibus quos circumducebat, lacerandos objicit.

Antonio de la Calancha, a Spanish official in Lima, wrote that during Vasco Núñez de Balboa's incursion across Panama, "he saw men dressed like women; Balboa learnt that they were sodomites and threw the king and forty others to be eaten by his dogs, a fine action of an honorable and Catholic Spaniard." (Guerra)

theaters in the U.S. at a time when Lou Dobbs and other white-supremacist propagandists are pitching classic fascist appeals to the middle-class in this country to view Mexican immigrants as "the enemy within."

It also screens as U.S. finance capital has unleashed its war machine to recolonize Iraq and Afghanistan under the banner of a "war on terror."

"Apocalypto" is pro-imperialist propaganda, making colonialism synonymous with salvation. The film ends with the Spanish fleet appearing on the horizon to save the day.

But when the lights come up, it is colonialism and imperialism that are the real historical "Apocalyptos."

Colonialism brings Inquisition

The patriarchs of colonial power violently restructured the Indigenous societies they militarily conquered—in economic organization, kinship, family/community organization, sexualities, gender and sex roles—in order to best facilitate enslavement, exploitation and oppression.

Mejía stated that with the arrival of the Spanish conquistadors, "An absolutist discourse enveloped homosexuality in the concepts of 'infamous sin,' 'sin against nature,' corruption of the soul and alliance with the devil. They punished the practice without distinctions, among both lay people and clerics."

This religious ideology and the ethos of male supremacy, he said, corresponded to the war-driven European social order.

"Furthermore," Mejía concludes, "the conquerors treated 'sodomy' as a special Indian sin and hunted it down and punished it as such on a grand scale. They orchestrated crusades like the Holy Inquisition, which began burning sodomites at the stake as a special occasion, as in the memorable auto-da-fé of San Lázaro in Mexico City."

This bloody crusade of terror is confirmed in the colonizers' own words.

Antonio de la Calancha, a Spanish official in Lima, wrote that during Vasco Núñez de Balboa's incursion across Panama, he "saw men dressed like women; Balboa learnt that they were sodomites and threw the king and forty others to be eaten by his dogs, a fine action of an honorable and Catholic Spaniard." (Guerra)

When the Spanish invaded the Antilles and Louisiana, "[T]hey found men dressed as women who were respected by their societies. Thinking they were hermaphrodites, or homosexuals, they slew them." (Green)

Native peoples throughout this hemisphere fought back.

Conquistador Nuño de Guzmán noted in 1530 that after one battle the last Indigenous person taken prisoner, who had "fought most courageously, was a man in the habit of a woman." (Burton) ▼

C. Robles was a one of a number of female-bodied Mexican revolutionaries who enlisted as males and fought for national independence from Spain. Robles and at least four others rose to the rank of colonel. (suppressedhistories.net).

Bodies shackled & repressed

Colonialism, and later imperialism, brought anti-homosexual and anti-trans laws and state repression to Cuba. The deep bite of the knotted lash of oppressor ideology backed them up.

For more than 300 years, Spanish colonialism shackled the laboring population of Cuba, literally claiming ownership of the lives, labor and bodies of millions.

The enslaved toilers were from the decimated Indigenous peoples of the island and African peoples—survivors of mass kidnappings from their homelands and of the Middle Passage holocaust.

Using Bibles as well as bullets, colonizers who bled the labor of the enslaved class literally "laid down the law"—reshaping and regulating every aspect of life for the enslaved class, including economic structure, kinship recognition, marriage, organization of the sexes, sexuality and gender expression.

Colonial terror, under the banner of religious law, enforced the brutal remodeling of economic and social life among peoples from diverse societies that the colonialists, and later imperialists, sought to conquer and exploit.

The following historical anecdote underscores the importance the colonial occupiers placed on eradicating the "pecado nefando"—the "nefarious sin" of same-sex love and/or gender/sex variance.

In order to petition Havana's town council in 1597 for his freedom, an enslaved man argued that he had "rendered a valuable service by discovering and denouncing those who had committed the 'pecado nefando.'" (de la Fuente)

There were many forms of resistance to colonial cultural imperialism. Santería, for example, used the trappings of Roman Catholicism to shelter African religious beliefs and rituals—which make room for very different sex/gender expression.

Havana: cross-dressing labor leader arrested

In the mid-1600s, the Spanish Captain General who ruled over the rural and urban enslaved population sentenced 20 "effeminate sodomites" to be burned to death.

Others were exiled to Cayo Cruz, a small island in Havana Bay, which was thereafter referred to in Spanish by an anti-homosexual slur.

Historian Amara Das Wilhelm added, "Similar disparaging attitudes toward homosexuals were expressed in a 1791 Havana newspaper article entitled 'A Critical Letter About the Man-Woman,' which condemned the effeminate sodomites that apparently thrived in eighteenth-century Havana." (The Gay and Lesbian Vaishnava Association online)

Revolutionary Puerto Rican trade unionist Luisa Capetillo on the day of her arrest in Havana on cross-dressing charges.

U.S. imperialism militarily occupied Cuba for four years, beginning in 1898. From 1902 until the 1959 Cuban Revolution, Wall Street ruled by establishing dictatorships to squeeze the island's economy in its fist, restructuring Cuba for exploitation as a giant sugar plantation.

Laws against same-sex love and gender variance and brutal state enforcement continued to be used as a cudgel for economic, social and political control.

Cross-dressing Puerto Rican labor organizer Luisa Capetillo was arrested in Havana in July 1915 for wearing men's clothing.

Capetillo was a single mother, a revolutionary, and a much-loved and respected labor organizer.

After supporting the 1905 farm workers' strike in the northern region of Puerto Rico, she became a reader in a tobacco plant, an industry whose workers were among the most politically conscious. She also spoke in public about the needs of working women, including the right to sex education. She strongly believed that sexuality was not the business of the church or the state.

As a full-time labor organizer after 1912, Capetillo traveled extensively, particularly to Havana, Tampa and New York because they were hubs of the tobacco workers' movement.

In Cuba, Capetillo actively supported a sugar cane workers' strike organized by the Anarchist Federation of Cuba.

The Cuban government tried unsuccessfully to deport her as an agitator.

Then it focused on her wearing of a "man's" suit, tie and fedora in public to charge her with "causing a scandal."

Capetillo fought the charge, arguing in court that no law prevented her from wearing men's garb, that such clothing was appropriate for the changing role of women in society, and that she had worn similar clothing in the streets of Puerto Rico and Mexico without state intervention.

Capetillo won her court battle—the judge ordered the charges dropped. News of her victory spread in articles in all the major newspapers in Cuba and Puerto Rico.

Historian Aurora Levins Morales concluded, "The incident received massive press coverage, and Capetillo used it as an opportunity to attack conventional morality, with its rigid sex roles, and women's imprisonment within it." (Morales)

In 1938, under U.S. domination, the Cuban Penal Code—the "Public Ostentation Law"—was enacted. This law mandated state penalties for "habitual homosexual acts," public displays of same-sex affection and/or gender-variant dress and self-expression.

▼

1950s Havana:
Imperialist sexploitation

For 450 years of Cuba's history, the social organization and state regulation of the sexes, gender expression and sexualities was—as among all occupied and colonized peoples—in thrall to the brutal systems of exploitation of agricultural landlords, capitalist bosses and imperialist finance capitalists.

By the mid-20th century, the impoverishment sweeping the island was the outgrowth of imperialism's conversion of the economy into sugar and citrus plantations and nickel mines that shackled the rural laboring population to the earth.

Havana exerted a gravitational pull on those who cut cane from sunup to sundown. By the 1950s, the promise of jobs attracted hundreds of thousands of impoverished rural workers of all sexualities, genders and sexes to the urban capital, the largest city on the island.

Many tens of thousands whose sexuality or gender expression had made them publicly vulnerable and without privacy in rural towns and villages found employment in Havana. Capitalist organized crime bosses ran an interlocking directorate of large-scale prostitution, tourism, gambling and drug distribution in the capital city.

In the 1950s, McCarthyite repression in the U.S.—including the puritanical purges and state repression carried out under the banner of fighting a "Lavender Menace"—spurred the expansion of this lucrative offshore capitalist sex-drugs-gambling industry in Havana for the rich and powerful to escape the U.S. Cold War climate.

"Not surprisingly, then," researchers Lourdes Arguelles and B. Ruby Rich stressed, "Cuban homosexuals had preferential hiring treatment in the Havana tourist sector in order to meet the demands" of U.S. businessmen and military brass.

Arguelles and Rich published their extensively researched report, entitled "Homosexuality, Homophobia, and Revolution: Notes Toward an Understanding of the Cuban Lesbian and Gay Male Experience," in the summer of 1984.

The two researchers added that the illegal prostitution industry was also created for the patriarchs and scions of the Cuban elite, who sought feminine male-bodied youth and adults.

In the towns and villages, sexuality, gender and the organization of the sexes were in the servitude of patriarchal agricultural servitude; in the urban capital, they were employed to meet the needs of patriarchal capitalist wage slavery.

Arguelles and Rich explained: "Even in the Havana of the 1950s, everyday life was not easy for the working-class or petty-bourgeois homosexual. Unemployment was high and had been steadily increasing throughout the decade. The scarcity of productive occupations demanded a strictly closeted occupational life. For all women, and especially for lesbians, employment almost invariably entailed continual sexual harassment."

Men who had sex with men and women who had sex with women were caught up in the dragnet of the illegal economy.

Arguelles and Rich noted: "Apart from employment realities, social pressures made thousands of pre-revolutionary homosexuals part of this underworld. Even homosexuals such as students (who were differently placed) were integrated into this subculture through the bars that they frequented: the St. Michel, the Dirty Dick, El Gato Tuerto." Most of these bars were owned by crime syndicates.

The researchers emphasized, "The commodification of homosexual desire in the Havana underworld and in the bourgeois homosexual underground during the pre-revolutionary era, however, did not produce a significant toleration of homosexual life-styles in the larger social arena.

"If legal sanctions and official harassment were rare," Arguelles and Rich explained, "this tolerance was due less to social acceptance than to overriding considerations of profit and the economic interests of the underworld that dominated the Cuban political apparatus.

"The consumer structure of the Havana underworld never spawned a 'gay culture' or 'gay sensibility' even in strictly commercial terms, due to its isolation from the mainstream of social life and the degree of guilt and self-hatred afflicting its members."

Arguelles and Rich concluded that Santería—African-Cuban religious beliefs and practices that challenge the colonialist and imperialist sex/gender and sexuality systems—has been a "favored form of gender transcendence for many Cuban homosexual men and lesbians." ▼

Why many Cuban gay men and lesbians left after 1959

Significant numbers of Cuban homosexual males and females, including many who were gender variant, began leaving the island immediately after the revolutionary 26th of July Movement overthrew the hated U.S.-backed Batista regime in 1959. The U.S. big-business media pointed their microphones at counter-revolutionary claims that anti-gay terror drove them to flee.

This reactionary political propaganda was a cover for a dirty war by imperialism to carry out "regime change" in Cuba. It also was aimed at demoralizing the multinational, revolutionary wing of the young gay liberation movement in the U.S.

This political and ideological campaign to paint Cuba as a cruel and oppressive dictatorship was crafted by Cold War capitalists who were themselves carrying out a ruthless domestic war against same-sex love and gender variance.

Before the Cuban Revolution, U.S. finance capital had installed two iron-fisted dictatorships in order to grease the gears of exploitation: Gerardo Machado in the late 1920s and Fulgencio Batista in the 1950s. For a cut of the profits, these brutal regimes served the rule of U.S. sugar, nickel and citrus companies and made it possible for the imperialists to own the banks, telephone and electric systems and big retail stores.

U.S. crime bosses ran the lucrative large-scale sex industry and interconnected casinos and drug distribution. Tens of thousands of Cuban women, men and children of all sexualities served the desires of wealthy and powerful tourists from the U.S.

Cold War anti-gay and anti-trans purges and persecution in the U.S. created the demand for an offshore prostitution network in Havana that exploited large numbers of men and boys, many of them feminine, for profit, as well as women.

The revolution that took state power on Jan. 1, 1959, shut down the sex industry and casinos. The workers—rural and urban—of Cuba faced a massive task: restructuring their economy to meet the needs of all, which meant creating jobs, introducing land reform, and providing food, clothing, housing, medical care, basic literacy and higher education.

This work had to be done while imperialism tried to take away every tool for change through economic strangulation, military encirclement and siege.

Seeking scientific understanding

Researchers Lourdes Arguelles and B. Ruby Rich made an important analytical contribution in the mid-1980s to understanding why many Cuban homosexuals left after the revolution—and why many stayed.

The two researchers took a scientific approach, accruing data through historical analysis, survey, field and experiential methods. They interpreted the results "within a theoretical framework drawn from lesbian-feminist and critical gay scholarship and the politico-economic and phenomenological study of Cuban social life."

Between 1979 and 1984 Arguelles and Rich interviewed Cubans on the island and émigrés in the United States, Spain, Mexico and Puerto Rico. The report on the research, titled "Homosexuality, Homophobia, and Revolution: Notes Toward an Understanding of the Cuban Lesbian and Gay Male Experience," was first published in the summer of 1984 in "Signs, A Journal of Women in Culture and Society."

The two researchers said their goals were to reveal the nature and dynamics of the Cuban homosexual experience in order to put the questions of same-sex love in Cuba, migration and resettlement in context.

They also sought to develop greater understanding of same-sex love in what were at that time referred to as Third World countries and communities, and to further develop theory "on the nature of the relationships between the structures of sexuality and the corresponding structures of socialist organization."

This is what they found.

Attempt to discredit the revolution

The role of economic incentive and individual ambition—powerful stimulants for all migration from poorer to wealthier countries—was seldom considered when it came to Cuban homosexual émigrés.

Arguelles and Rich wrote, "The more structuralist explanations for international population movements, which stress the role of capital and of capitalist states in organizing migratory flows from less developed to more developed economies, have yet to be invoked in the interpretation of gay migration from Cuba."

Washington had passed the Immigration and Naturalization Act in 1952, which specifically mandated blocking entry of/or expelling "sexually deviant" immigrants. But when it came to Cuban homosexuals, Arguelles and Rich noted, "Then, as now, anticommunism won out."

Wealthy homosexual male Cubans, who before the revolution had spent extensive periods abroad, left the island for good. "Emigration began immediately. The promoters and overlords of the Havana underworld along with large numbers of their displaced workers (many of them homosexuals) headed for Miami. Many lesbians who had liaisons with members of the bourgeoisie followed their male protectorate to Miami, as did gay men who had worked for U.S. firms or had done domestic work for the native bourgeoisie."

The two researchers point out that Cuban "refugee" testimony became "the main source for evaluation of Cuban gay life, despite knowledge of the pressures on émigrés to testify to political persecution in their country of origin in order to attain the legal and economic advantages of refugee status in their new country."

These narratives were then amplified as part of an imperialist propaganda campaign calculated to neutralize "badly needed support for the Cuban revolution among its natural allies," Arguelles and Rich wrote. In addition, the propaganda campaign "legitimated the presence in traditionally liberal circles of some of the more reactionary elements within the Cuban émigré population."

They added that this propaganda obscured changing realities of gay life in Cuba as part of the ongoing revolutionary process, made the historical inheritance of the pre-revolutionary political economy and homophobia seem irrelevant, and helped to disguise the oppression and exploitation of gay and lesbian Cubans living in émigré enclaves.

The campaign also distanced "gay activists in capitalist mainstream culture from minority gays involved in the liberation movements of their respective countries and national communities."

And lastly, this scapegoating of Cuba "has made the growing number of progressive gay émigrés who criticize but also support the revolution into living contradictions: invisible to gay liberation forces but easy targets for the homophobic anti-Castro army in exile."

While many left the island, many others stayed.

Arguelles and Rich concluded, "Other homosexuals, especially those from working-class backgrounds or students from petty-bourgeois families, worked to integrate themselves into the revolution."

They stressed, "For these homosexuals, class and class interests were perceived as more elemental aspects of their identity than homosexual behavior. And the revolution spoke to these interests and this identity."

There was work for all, free health care, free education, affordable housing and tremendous cultural growth.

Cuban lesbians, some of whom had played an important role in the pre-revolutionary urban struggle, also benefited from the great gains being made by and for women. ▼

Early Cuban Revolution
paved road to sexual liberation

The first revolutionary step toward the liberation of sexuality, gender expression and oppressed sexes in Cuba was the dismantling of the sex-for-profit industry and interconnected gambling dens and drug-distribution networks. This concrete, material first act by the Cuban Revolution unshackled human bodies, desire and gender expression from capitalist commodification, commercialization and exploitation.

For almost half a millennium the island had been manacled by colonialism, capitalism and imperialism. The holds of their ships brought enslaved peoples from Africa. Their advanced weaponry was cocked and trained on the enslaved laborers. The ideological lash of the Roman Catholic Church sliced to the bone. White supremacist, racist ideology, patriarchal oppression of women and state-enforced repression against same-sex love ruled the economic and social order.

Just as colonialism and imperialism left the island's fertile soil cultivated as a single-crop plantation, class enslavement tilled the fields of culture.

When the revolutionary process began, it had to start from there.

Before the 1959 revolution, the burgeoning sector of the Cuban economy was Havana's prostitution industry, booming with Cold War consumption—the largest in the Caribbean—and the gambling, drugs and tourism connected to it. U.S. crime syndicate bosses and wealthy Cubans with connections to Batista's regime owned the profitable operations.

Arguelles and Rich noted that this illegal economy "employed more than two hundred thousand workers as petty traders, casino operators, entertainers, servants and prostitutes." (Arguelles)

Many were homosexual—male and female—and many of the males were feminine. Crime bosses also exploited tens of thousands of heterosexual women and men in the prostitution industry. All performed to the sexual whims of the fathers and sons of the U.S. and Cuban ruling classes.

Cuban citizen, translator and interpreter Leonardo Hechavarría, and Cuban defender, typographer and gay rights activist Marcel Hatch, summed up that era: "Before the 1959 Revolution, life for lesbians and gays was one of extreme isolation and repression, enforced by civil law, augmented by Catholic dogma. Patriarchal attitudes made lesbians invisible. If discovered, they'd often suffer sexual abuse, disgrace in the community, and job loss.

"Havana's gay male underground—some 200,000—was a purgatory of prostitution to American tourists, domestic servitude, and constant threats of violence and blackmail." (Hatch)

Arguelles and Rich explained: "It was just a profitable commodification of sexual fantasy. For the vast majority, homosexuality made life a shameful and guilt-ridden experience. Such was gay Havana in the fabled 'avant la guerre' period."

Reactionaries prey on dislocation

For male homosexuals in Havana, particularly those who were feminine and/or cross-dressing, social outlets for congregating were limited once this large-scale illegal economy was shut down after the revolution.

As a result, Arguelles and Rich explained, this "prolonged the relationship between the declining underworld and more progressive homosexuals, locking the two groups together for sheer companionship and sexual pleasure."

That was truer for Cuban males than females.

The two researchers also noted, "Homosexual perspectives on the revolution could shift according to class interests."

Middle-class homosexuals whose privileges were threatened by agrarian and urban reforms banded, they said, with "the remaining veterans of the underworld" to oppose the revolution.

"Some veterans of the old underworld enclave joined counter-revolutionary activities or were pushed into them by the CIA," Arguelles and Rich reported. "Not a few of the progressive homosexuals became implicated by default in counter-revolutionary activities and were even jailed.

"Young homosexuals seeking contact with 'the community' in the bars and famous cruising areas of La Rampa were thus introduced to counter-revolutionary ideology and practice. One example of such a dynamic is the case of Rolando Cubela, a homosexual student leader who fought in the revolutionary army but was later enlisted by the CIA to assassinate Fidel Castro."

The two researchers concluded, "Homosexual bars and La Rampa cruising areas were perceived, in some cases correctly, as centers of counter-revolutionary activities and began to be systematically treated as such."

Cuban women organize for gains

The overall situation for Cuban women who loved women had its own characteristics.

Under the triple weight of the patriarchies of colonialism, capitalism and imperialism, a dynamic women's movement emerged in Cuba as early as the 1920s and Cuban women won the right to vote and be elected to public office in 1934. (thegully.com)

After the 1959 seizure of state power, it was Cuban women as a whole who became the driving force to break the chokehold of centuries-old patriarchal economic and social organization, and the attitudes about women and femininity it engendered.

The Cuban Women's Federation (FMC) formed quickly after the revolution in 1960. It exerted immeasurably more power because it was a part of the revolution, not apart from it.

At a 1966 leadership meeting of the FMC, President Fidel Castro observed, "Women's participation in the revolution was a revolution in the revolution, and if we were asked what the most revolutionary thing that the revolution is doing, we would answer that it is precisely this—the revolution that is occurring among the women of our country." (Hillson)

Hechavarría and Hatch stressed, "Following the Revolution, women won near full equality under the law, including pay equity, the right to child care, abortion, and military service, among other historic gains, laying the basis for their higher social and political status.

"This foundation, a first in the Americas, played an important role in women's greater independence and sexual freedom, a prerequisite for homosexual liberation. The Revolution also destroyed the Mafia-controlled U.S. tourist driven prostitution trade that held many Cuban women and gay men in bondage."

Hechavarría and Hatch added, "The Revolution undertook to provide ample education and employment opportunities for female prostitutes.

"Advances for women in general were naturally extended to lesbians, and many became among the most ardent defenders of the Revolution."

Revolutionizing the sexes

Cuban men, as well as women, had been treated as the property of other men—the patriarchs of property.

Revolutionary Cuban men have carried out their own work to consciously build the consciousness of a "new man" on the basis of new social principles.

Ché Guevara, Fidel Castro and the Cuban Revolution as a whole challenged all Cuban men to examine male consciousness, attitudes and behaviors.

This revolutionary effort, which continues today, aimed to change old ways that men were taught to interact with women. Like the revolution itself, this work is most profoundly meaningful because it is a process, not a single act.

The revolution challenged the biology-is-destiny "natural order" ideologies of colonialism, capitalism and imperialism that elevated patriarchs to rule.

The revolution challenged the reactionary biological determinist concept that men are innately superior and women are naturally submissive.

But genuine economic and social equality for women, and profound change of the attitudes of men, could only be generated by economic and social reorganization that could lift the standard of living for all. Imperialism was determined to thwart and sabotage that work at every moment. U.S. finance capital cinched the island in an economic noose, and the Pentagon cordoned the island, attacking overtly and covertly.

As Washington and the Pentagon ratcheted up the pressure on Cuba, and the CIA spearheaded the commando invasion at Playa Girón, the entire island's population had to be organized and mobilized to meet two huge tasks—military defense of the revolution and harvest of the cane crop that sustained economic life.

Everyone—of all sexes, genders and sexualities, from children to elders—was called up for these life-and-death tasks.

Inside Cuba, trying to fit many thousands of urban homosexual and/or gender-variant males into agricultural work sharpened a social contradiction.

Outside Cuba, propagandistic exploitation of this contradiction led to one of the worst slanders against the Cuban Revolution in the history of the workers' state. ▼

1965 UMAP brigades:
What they were, what they were not

One of the most terrible slanders against the Cuban Revolution is that the workers' state was a "penal colony," interning gay men in "concentration camps" in 1965. That charge, which refers to the 1965 mobilization of Units to Aid Military Production (UMAP), still circulates today as good coin.

Therefore the formation and ending of the UMAP work brigades in the history of the Cuban workers' state is vitally important for today's activists to study very carefully and thoroughly. Those who are working hard to make a revolution in the heartland of imperialism will pay the most careful attention, and bring the most genuine solidarity and humility—teachability—to this important analysis.

For those worldwide who struggle against oppression based on sexuality, gender and sex, the sharpening of this sexual/gender/sex contradiction in Cuba in 1965 offers this critical lesson: The way sexuality and the sexes are socially organized, and gender is socially assigned and allowed to be expressed, always has a history.

Since the overturning of matrilineal, cooperative societies, strict organization based on race, sex, gender expression and sexuality has served the dictates of ruling-class economic organization, and has been under the knuckles of state regulation and repression.

Pre-revolutionary Cuba was no exception.

Spain exports Inquisition

Without understanding Cuba's historical process, it's impossible to understand its revolutionary process.

Researcher Ian Lumsden noted in his study on Cuba and homosexuality, "There is much speculation about the incidence of homosexual activity between Cuba's indigenous people, as there is with respect to other parts of the New World. Whatever its true extent, it was used as a pretext for Spain to enslave natives on the grounds that they were not fully human."

He explained that, "Condemnation of sodomy and subsequently of homosexuality, along with repressive mystification of women's sexuality, have long been at the core of Spanish Catholic dogmas regarding sexuality." Only crimes against the king and heresy were higher crimes than "sodomy" in the Middle Ages.

Lumsden added, "There was competition between the Inquisition and the secular courts about who should have authority to exorcise it from the body politic."

Sentences ranged from castration to being burned alive.

The domestic Spanish crusade against "sodomy," he explained, was driven by the ruling class "desire to expunge Moorish cultural influence from Spain, which they associated, among other things, with homosexual and cross-dressing behavior."

Pivotal impact of slavery

Lumsden paraphrased, "As Julio Le Riverend, Cuba's leading economic historian, reminds us, the development of Cuba, particularly since the 18th century, cannot be understood without recognizing the pivotal impact of slavery as a mode of production on all social relations, including domestic ones. Homosexuality among slaves occurred in a context—that is, a country whose dominant culture was both racist and homophobic."

The system of plantation slavery—both chattel and latifundia—created rural enslavement in which the masters on the island, and the masters across the Florida Straits, claimed to own the bodies and lives and labor of enslaved workers.

The patriarchal slave-masters, landowners and their overseers dictated the clothing enslaved workers could wear; where they could live and in what arrangements; when the sexes could meet; where, when and how they could have sex; if they could marry and, if so, who they could marry.

Of the more than 40,000 Asian laborers counted in the 1871 Cuban census, for example, only 66 were women and the law forbade Chinese males from marrying African-Cubans.

Enslaved African males outnumbered females by a ratio of almost two to one. Males were often housed together in isolated regions in single-sex barracones—plantation barracks—in which no women were allowed.

In his oral narrative, former enslaved African laborer Esteban Montejo told Miguel Barnet about men routinely coupling with other men in everyday life in the barracones. And he offered a glimpse at how they were gendered in relation to each other. Montejo only refers to the partner who looks after a *marido* (husband) as what the Spanish would term "sodomite." (Lumsden)

Montejo said it was only "after slavery that [the] word *afeminado* appeared."

Centralization and commodification

Capitalism and imperialism did not create homosexuality or gender variance in Cuba; these market forces centralized, commodified and commercialized them.

Rural poverty made capitalist relations—the often empty promise of jobs—a magnet that drew hundreds of thousands of campesin@s from the impoverished countryside to the cities, in particular the capital Havana, in search of wage work.

"During this period of severe sexual repression in advanced capitalist nations," Arguelles and Rich explained, "homosexual desire was often channeled into illegal and lucrative offshore markets like the Havana underworld."

The crime syndicates and wealthy Cubans with ties to the Batista dictatorship gave "preferential hiring" to Cuban homosexuals, many of them feminine and/or cross-dressing males, to serve the demand of the dollar, and those whose wallets were filled with cash.

"Other buyers of homosexual desire," Arguelles and Rich elaborated, "were the fathers and sons of the Cuban bourgeoisie, who felt free to partake of homoerotic practices without being considered homosexual as long as they did not take the passive, so-called female role in sexual relations. Yet another common practice for Cuban heterosexual men was the procurement of a lesbian prostitute's favors for a night."

Poverty drew many heterosexual Cuban men "into this underworld or alternatively into a homosexual underground dominated by the Cuban homosexual bourgeoisie," the two researchers added. The bourgeois Cuban male homosexual of this era sought out masculine men from the laboring class.

"Thus," Arguelles and Rich observed, "in many ways, pre-revolutionary homosexual liaisons in themselves fostered sexual colonialism and exploitation."

Overall, the pre-revolutionary state regulated this sex-for-profit industry, rather than repress it.

Fidel: 'We were forced to mobilize'

Shutting down the exploitative economic industries in Havana after seizure of state power was just one revolutionary task. Building a planned, productive economy that could meet the needs of 9 million urban and rural workers was a whole other job—and a difficult one, at that.

"Let me tell you about the problems we had," Cuban revolutionary leader Fidel Castro recalled. "In those first years we were forced to mobilize the whole nation because of the risks we were facing, which included that of an attack by the United States: the dirty war, the Bay of Pigs invasion, the Missile Crisis." (Ramonet)

Fidel Castro talked extensively about the UMAP in two interviews. The first was in a conversation with Tomás Borge, published in "Face to Face with Fidel Castro" (Ocean Press: 1992). The second was in conversations between 2003 and 2005 with Ignacio Ramonet, published by the Cuban Council of State in April 2006.

Recalling the period of 1965, Castro outlined three obstacles in organizing this island-wide emergency mobilization to defend the revolution and to build the economy. The first two: The CIA was beaming messages to entice skilled workers and technicians to emigrate. And members of Catholic, Jehovah's Witnesses and Seventh-Day Adventist religious organizations would not take up arms in defense of the island. (Ramonet)

"[A]t the triumph of the Revolution," President Castro explained, "the stage we are speaking of, the [male chauvinist] element was very much present, together with widespread opposition to having homosexuals in military units." (Ramonet)

The Cuban leader said that as a result, "Homosexuals were not drafted at first, but then all that became a sort of irritation factor, an argument some people used to lash out at homosexuals even more.

"Taking those three categories into account we founded the so-called Military Units to Support Production (UMAP) where we sent people from the said three categories: those whose educational level was insufficient; those who refused to serve out of religious convictions; or homosexuals who were physically fit. Those were the facts; that's what happened.

"Those units were set up all throughout the country for purposes of work, mainly to assist agriculture. That is, homosexuals were not the only ones affected, though many of them certainly were, not all of them, just those who were called to do mandatory service in the ranks, since it was an obligation and everyone was participating." (Ramonet)

Sexual, gender contradictions sharpened

Revolutionary reorganization in Cuba in 1965, staring down the barrel of imperialism's cannons, had to reintegrate a numerically large homosexual/transgender population from the cities back into the rural agricultural production.

This returning workforce from the capitalist urban center had to go back to the rural agricultural production that many had left earlier in their lives.

When large numbers of feminine homosexual males returned to the countryside from Havana, it was not just a conflict of differently socialized sexual expression, but a collision between historically differently gendered workforces.

Capitalist relations had consolidated the sex-for-profit industry which had given mass expression to homosexuality and feminine expression in males, and shaped these as commodities on the auction block of the market.

The urban homosexual/gender-variant cultures, dress, mores and social semaphores seemed to many Cubans—even men who had sex with men and women who had sex with women—to have washed up on the island's shores on the waves of oppressive and exploitative capitalist and imperialist cultures.

Arguelles and Rich stressed that at the time of the revolution, "Erotic loyalty (and, in the case of women, subservience) to the opposite sex was assumed as normal even by homosexuals. Hence, for many Cubans of this era, homosexuality was a mere addendum to customary marital roles. Among others, it was just a profitable commodification of sexual fantasy. For the vast majority, homosexuality made life a shameful and guilt-ridden experience."

Fidel Castro stressed that the UMAP "were not internment units, nor were they punishment units; on the contrary, it was about morale, to give them a chance to work and help the country in those difficult circumstances. Besides, there were many who for religious reasons had the chance to help their homeland in another way by serving not in combat units but in work units." (Ramonet)

President Castro cut cane; children worked in the fields. Renowned Cubans such as musician and poet Pablo Milanés and Baptist pastor and MP Raúl Suárez worked in the UMAP. And they stayed to help build the revolution.

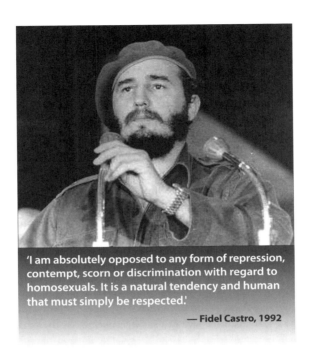

'I am absolutely opposed to any form of repression, contempt, scorn or discrimination with regard to homosexuals. It is a natural tendency and human that must simply be respected.'

— Fidel Castro, 1992

The whole island was hard at work building an independent existence, in economic soil deeply furrowed by the plows of colonialism and imperialism.

Fidel shut down the UMAP

Fidel Castro stated categorically about the UMAP, "I can tell you for sure that there was prejudice against homosexuals." (Ramonet)

On the island, the Cuban National Union of Artists and Writers (UNEAC) reportedly protested treatment of homosexuals working in UMAP, prompting Fidel Castro to check it out for himself. (Hillson)

A Cuban who worked in a UMAP, interviewed by Nicaraguan poet Ernesto Cardenal in 1970-1971, related that Fidel slipped into a UMAP brigade one night and lay down in one of the hammocks. The interviewee said that the UMAP guards would sometimes cut the hammock cords with their sabers. "When one guard raised his saber he found himself staring at Fidel; he almost dropped dead. Fidel is the man of the unexpected visits." (Cardenal)

A youth described as a "young Marxist revolutionary" told Cardenal that 100 young males from the Communist Youth were sent to the UMAP to report back about how homosexuals were treated. "It was a highly secret operation. Not even their families knew of this plan. Afterward the boys told what had happened. And they put an end to the UMAP." (Hillson)

One youth concluded to Cardenal, "[W]e who were in the UMAP discovered that the Revolution and the UMAP were separable. And we said to ourselves: We won't leave Cuba, we'll stay and make what is bad not bad." (Hillson)

Fidel: 'Overcoming legacy of chauvinism'

Fidel Castro explained that during this period of early revolutionary history, "Concerning women, there was a strong prejudice, as strong as in the case of homosexuals. I'm not going to come up with excuses now, for I assume my share of the responsibility. I truly had other concepts regarding that issue." (Ramonet)

"I am not going to deny that, at one point, male chauvinism also influenced our attitude toward homosexuality," he said. (Borge)

"We inherited male chauvinism and many other bad habits from the conquistadors. I would say that it corresponded to a given stage and is largely associated with that legacy of chauvinism." (Borge)

Castro stressed, "Homosexuals were certainly discriminated against—more so in other countries—but it happened here too, and fortunately our people, who are far more cultured and learned now, have gradually left that prejudice behind. (Ramonet)

"We have made a real advance—we can see it, especially in the young people, but we can't say that sexual discrimination has been completely wiped out and we mustn't lower our guard." (Borge)

He said, "I must also tell you that there were—and there are—extremely outstanding personalities in the fields of culture and literature, famous names this country takes pride in, who were and still are homosexual.

"Today the people have acquired a general, rounded culture. I'm not going to say there is no male chauvinism, but now it's not anywhere near the way it was back then, when that culture was so strong. With the passage of years and the growth of consciousness about all of this, we have gradually overcome problems and such prejudices have declined. But believe me, it was not easy." (Ramonet)

Fidel Castro concluded in 1992: "I am absolutely opposed to any form of repression, contempt, scorn or discrimination with regard to homosexuals. It is a natural tendency and human that must simply be respected." (Borge) ▼

Hollywood projected Cuba as 'police state' for gays

Hollywood turned up the volume on charges that Cuba was a "penal colony" for homosexual males with its release of "Before Night Falls" in August 2000.

The movie was based on a memoir by the late anti-communist Cuban homosexual writer Reinaldo Arenas, who emigrated to the United States in 1980. A decade later Arenas committed suicide in a dilapidated Hell's Kitchen apartment in Manhattan, the capital of capital. Impoverished and dying as a result of AIDS, he had no health insurance and could not afford high medical costs of care—rights enjoyed by every Cuban under the revolution in his homeland.

Since the early days of the 1959 revolution, the CIA had trolled for grievances about the revolution—real, manufactured or exaggerated.

"Before Night Falls" was the pinnacle of this propaganda campaign, by virtue of having the most capital invested in its production, its cast and distribution network; the publicity generated for its release; and the accolades and awards that gave it the imprimatur of "truth." Interspersed snippets of actual archival footage from the early days of the revolution and snippets of newsreel of Fidel Castro's speeches aim to lend the film the appearance of historical authenticity.

As the movie begins, the cameras pan across what is actually rural Mexico, as the backdrop for Arenas' childhood in Cuba. The reality of agricultural plantation enslavement is nowhere to be seen. Instead, the voiceover narrates that the author's childhood was "splendor," adding that "it was absolute poverty but also absolute freedom … ."

Projected onto movie screens, "Before Night Falls" became an imperialist-era sequel to "Gone with the Wind."

In both reactionary propaganda films, bygone epochs of white-supremacist plantation slavery—which shackled African and Indigenous peoples—are nostalgically revived, revised and romanticized. In both films, the armies that break the manacles of slavery for profit are cast as the bad guys.

Pre-revolution: exploitation, not freedom

Viewers of "Before Night Falls" are left with the overall impression that the U.S.-backed Batista regime actually offered greater "freedom."

In an October 2001 movie review about "Before Night Falls," entitled "Gays in Cuba, from the Hollywood School of Falsification," Leonardo Hechavarría and Marcel Hatch took on this fiction.

Hechavarría's biography describes him as a Cuban citizen, a translator and interpreter, and states that "he is a passionate advocate of the Revolution and works for increased acceptance of lesbians and gays in his homeland." Marcel Hatch is identified as a typographer, "a veteran gay rights activist and Cuba defender."

Hechavarría and Hatch wrote: "Before the 1959 Revolution, life for lesbians and gays was one of extreme isolation and repression, enforced by civil law, augmented by Catholic dogma. Patriarchal attitudes made lesbians invisible. If discovered, they'd often suffer sexual abuse, disgrace in the community and job loss.

"Havana's gay male underground—some 200,000—was a purgatory of prostitution to American tourists, domestic servitude and constant threats of violence and blackmail. The closet was the operative image. Survival often meant engaging in fake heterosexual marriage, or banishment to the gay slum."

For more analysis of "Before Night Falls," also see "The Sexual Politics of Reinaldo Arenas: Fact, Fiction and the Real Record of the Cuban Revolution," by Jon Hillson, at www.blythe.org.

Arguelles and Rich noted about life for the homosexual/transgender urban work force in pre-revolutionary Cuba, "If legal sanctions and official harassment were rare, this tolerance was due less to social acceptance than to overriding considerations of profit and the economic interests of the underworld that dominated the Cuban political apparatus."

But the misery of urban sexual enslavement in brothels, casinos, domestic work and drug networking is nowhere to be seen in "Before Night Falls." Neither is the apparatus of the Batista dictatorship's police, secret agents and army.

Workers' state, not bosses' state

"Before Night Falls" is the blockbuster of the propagandistic charges that the Cuban Revolution ushered in a "police state," similar to fascist Nazi Germany and the bloody 1973 counter-revolution in Chile.

These vilifications purposely confused the difference between a workers' state and a bosses' state. Understanding the class character of the Cuban workers' state is very important for those who seek their own liberation today.

Cuba was a newly developing workers' state—which had to literally battle overt and covert military onslaught and economic strangulation by U.S. imperialism. At the same time the revolution had to fight the legacy of racist, sexist and anti-homosexual/transgender indoctrination by patriarchal colonialism, capitalism and imperialism.

In contrast, the state machineries of the exploiting classes—and the church hierarchies that serve them—have always relied on repressive terror, and deepening and strengthening homophobia and transphobia, in order to conquer and rule.

For example, the Spanish colonial state in Cuba enslaved the Indigenous population on the island, castrated those it considered "sodomites," and forced them to eat their own testicles coated with dirt. (Iznada)

In order to save German capitalism, a wing of industrialists and bankers bankrolled the fascists who forced tens of thousands of gays and lesbians to wear the pink triangle in slave labor and extermination camps.

Víctor Hugo Robles wrote of Chile—where the mass of workers and peasants were not armed against the 1973 CIA-backed counter-revolution—that, "Perhaps the most forgotten are the many transvestites who were executed during the days immediately following the coup." ("The Homosexual Liberation Movement in Chile")

In the imperialist United States, homosexuality and sex/gender variance were so viciously criminalized and punished by state repression that a mass political movement arose to resist it. Despite widespread struggle, same-sex love remained illegal in the United States until 2003. Currently, in 2007, at least 65 percent of transwomen and 29 percent of transmen are estimated to have been imprisoned at some point in their life in the United States. (Critical Resistance)

And today it is U.S. imperialism that has set up concentration camps—from Abu Ghraib to Guantánamo—where anti-gay and anti-trans rape and humiliation are incorporated into the science of torture.

The state of former slaves

The Cuban workers' state, like the armies of Bolívar and Toussaint L'Ouverture, is an armed liberation struggle of the oppressed against the Goliath force of the oppressor state.

An estimated 20,000 Cubans died in two years of battling the U.S.-backed Batista dictatorship—up against bombs, aircraft and artillery. The revolution disarmed the Batista regime's army and secret police networks.

However, simply dismantling the bosses' apparatus of dictatorship did not create a new mechanism to defend the island from counter-revolution and invasion. Imperialism soon cinched an economic noose around the island, its Pentagon a constant threat.

A new state had to be built, from the ground up. It took a mass mobilization of the population to defend the gains of the revolution. The National Revolutionary Militia and the Committees for the Defense of the Revolution organized the entire population into a network against CIA-organized subterfuge and sabotage.

This block-by-block watchfulness, combined with old, deep prejudice against same-sex liaisons, made life uncomfortable for some Cuban male homosexuals. While they had experienced extreme isolation and alienation in the sexual exploitation industry, they had also found refuge in urban anonymity and privately-owned casinos, bars and other meeting places.

However, unlike its portrayal in "Before Night Falls," the Cuban workers' state was not a repressive apparatus. Rather, it had the task of defending 11 million Cubans from re-enslavement by U.S. finance capital. The Cuban Revolution could not have survived a day, let alone a half century, without organizing and mobilizing the population to defend its independence from imperialism.

The Committees for the Defense of the Revolution and the Cuban popular militias— which armed millions of women as well as men—are the protective might of a formerly enslaved population against enraged former plantation owners, bankers, industrialists and syndicate bosses.

Arming the Cuban population of workers—rural and urban—made it possible to defeat the invasion at Playa Girón (the Bay of Pigs). At the same time, this defense allowed the revolution to boot out the U.S. sugar plantation owners and give the land back to those who tilled it. It allowed the revolution to oust U.S. industrialists and bankers, and crime syndicate bosses who ran the lucrative brothel, gambling and drug networks. The revolution began deconstructing the white supremacist and patriarchal systems that hadn't allowed Cubans of African descent to set foot on the beaches, and had kept women in servitude.

This was a workers' state.

'Dispute this fable with facts'

Calling for an end to Hollywood's blockade of Cuba, Hechavarría and Hatch stressed about "Before Night Falls": "[I]n a queer cinemagraphic twist, it erases the achievements of Cuban toilers, women, people of color, and indeed gays, who've made stupendous advances since 1959.

"The end of hunger, homelessness, illiteracy, high infant mortality, and foreign domination of the island are of course undeniable—all fruits of the Revolution."

After the revolution, "advances for women in general were naturally extended to lesbians, and many became among the most ardent defenders of the revolution. On the other hand, a significant minority of gay men left Cuba. Some joined the counter-revolutionary expatriates in Miami or were blackmailed into doing so. Ironically, the U.S., which was busy flushing out and jailing its homosexuals during the McCarthy period, welcomed Cuban gays as part of its overall campaign to destabilize the island." (Hatch)

Hechavarría and Hatch added: "It was Clinton/Bush [Sr.]-inspired destiny that a hot button pushing, gay-themed anti-Cuba melodrama would be released. The persistent myth, promulgated chiefly by right-wing Cuban-Americans (most of whom are hyper-homophobes), that homosexuality is illegal in Cuba, that gays and lesbians are banned from the Communist Party, and that they are savaged and tossed in the slammer, is pure bunk."

Hechavarría and Hatch stated categorically: "We know of no Cuban, for or against their government, who finds the movie credible. Nor do smart gay activists.

"This political falsity," they concluded, "has widespread currency among liberal skeptics and within the queer community [in the U.S.] It is to this audience the film was targeted. It is necessary for friends of Cuba to dispute this fable with facts." ▼

1970s: Decade of cultural progress

Those who today are working to seize state power and defend and build a workers' state in their own countries may be sobered as well as heartened by the enormous cultural labor that the Cuban Revolution had to accomplish in the 1970s, particularly regarding liberation of women, sexuality and gendered social roles.

Arguelles and Rich concluded in their 1984 study of Cuba that three events "marked the gradual but continual improvement of life conditions of gay men and lesbians in Cuba during the seventies: the First National Congress on Education and Culture, the promulgation of the Family Code, and the creation of a national group on sexual education."

Arguelles and Rich explain that at the 1971 Congress on Education and Culture, "On the one hand, homosexuality was not referred to as a product of decadence and homosexuality was no longer seen by the revolutionary leadership as a fundamental problem in Cuban society, but, rather, viewed as a form of sexual behavior requiring study.

"On the other hand, declarations from the same congress called for the removal of homosexuals from the field of education, thus continuing the view of homosexuality as a contamination of the body politic."

The 1971 congress declaration demoralized some activists worldwide who had hoped that the seizure of state power in Cuba would usher in an immediate and thorough-going theoretical, social and economic transformation.

Some activists succumbed to fear that prejudice is a hard-wired human trait that can't ever be eradicated from any human society, even a socialist one.

Anti-communists have also tried to use the 1971 congress document in attempts to discredit the revolutionary process altogether.

Both are ample reason to look more closely.

Roots of prejudice

Studying Cuba's specific historical economic and social conditions opens up greater understanding about what generates prejudice against same-sex love and gender variance, as well as racism, and opens up clarity about what kind of material changes are necessary to eventually uproot all forms of bigotry.

Prejudice—ideology that pits groups within the vast laboring and oppressed class worldwide against each other—is not the same as superstition. Superstitions are explanations concerning the material world that the scientific process later proves are untrue.

Attempts to supplant that new, scientific understanding with old superstitions are consciously reactionary.

Prejudices, however, are rooted in the historical development of class-divided societies. They are used as a conscious ideological campaign to frustrate mass unity among the laboring masses over millennia. These lies, minted like gold, have only profited emperors and kings, landowners and barons.

"The ideas of the ruling class are in every epoch the ruling ideas," observed Karl Marx, "i.e., the class which is the ruling material force of society, is at the same time its ruling intellectual force."

Colonialism and imperialism didn't just bring reactionary ideas. The patriarchal ruling-class ideologies they enforced served to buttress their structures of enslavement of Cuba, as elsewhere.

Spanish colonialism backed up its edicts against same-sex love in Cuba with Inquisition terror, and its church imbued this sexuality with shame and guilt.

Imperialism swiftly centralized and shaped what became a numerically huge new urban homosexual/gender-variant subculture, mostly male, within the larger culture(s) in Cuba for the sole purpose of sexual exploitation for profit. Tens of thousands of Cuban women and girls, including many enslaved in "domestic" jobs, were ruthlessly sexually exploited, as well.

So it is not difficult to understand why homosexuality, coupled with gender variance, would seem to be a product of "bourgeois decadence" in Cuba. And it's not hard to understand why many Cubans believed that homosexuality and gender varience would go away with the shutting down of these non-productive, exploitative industries.

But the 1971 cultural congress marked the moving away from that assumption.

Changing ideas

Revolution is not a single act, it's a process. The revolution created the basis for social and economic transformation that has been profound and is ongoing, a particularly remarkable achievement carried out under almost half a century of imperialist siege.

The first tasks of the revolution in Cuba were to organize to provide jobs, food, shelter, health care and education for the entire population and to defend the new revolutionary state against imperialist attack.

At the same time, the 1959 Cuban Revolution faced the odious task of cleaning out the Augean stables filled with 450 years of rotting, stinking oppressor culture excreted by Spanish colonialism and U.S. imperialism. And the U.S. tried to take away every shovel that the Cubans needed to do that work.

While deep divisions based on bigotry help facilitate and maintain colonial and imperialist economic rule, every form of ideological prejudice—white supremacy, male supremacy and anti-homosexual bigotry—breaks up the unity required to collectively build a socialist economy.

The 1971 congress declaration pointed out that, "For the bourgeoisie, the elimination of the cultural elements of its class and system represents the elimination of culture as such.

"For the working class and people in general, the culture born of the revolutionary struggle is the conquest and development of the most valuable of humanity's cultural heritage which the exploiters kept from them for centuries."

The 1971 congress declaration stressed that "[T]he changes in the field of sexual relations stem from society itself as it progresses in the social, cultural and economic fields and continues to acquire an ideology that is more consistently revolutionary."

Fidel: 'tangible and practical successes'

Looking back from the vantage point of 1992, Cuban revolutionary leader Fidel Castro told Tomás Borge, a priest and founder of the Sandinista National Liberation Front, "We inherited male chauvinism and many other bad habits from the conquistadors. That was an historical inheritance. In some countries more than in others, but in none was there more struggle than in ours and I believe that in none have there been more tangible and practical successes." (Borge)

Fidel Castro recalled, in a series of interviews between 2003 and 2005, "[W]e had to work very hard to do away with racial prejudice here. Concerning women, there was strong prejudice, as strong as in the case of homosexuals." (Ramonet)

Castro had told Borge, "There was, for example, one standard for judging the personal conduct of a man and another for a woman. We had this situation for years in the party and I led fights and argued a lot about this. If there was infidelity in a marriage on behalf of the man, there was no problem, no worry, on the other hand it was a subject of discussion in the party units when there was infidelity on the part of the woman. There was one way of judging sexual relations of men and another of women. I had to fight hard, against deeply rooted tendencies that were not the product of any sermon or doctrine, or education, but the male chauvinist concepts and prejudices that exist in the heart of our society."

Castro added, "I am not going to deny that, at one point, male chauvinism also influenced our attitudes towards homosexuality."

He explained to Ramonet, "There was less prejudice against homosexuals in the most cultured and educated sectors, but that prejudice was very strong in sectors of low educational level—the illiteracy rate was around 30 percent those years—and among the nearly-illiterate, and even among many professionals. That was a real fact in our society." (Ramonet)

One of the first actions of the revolution in 1960—the Year of Education—was to organize volunteers to teach 700,000 adults to read. Cuba rapidly reached the highest literacy rate in Latin America.

Fidel Castro metaphorically answered the idealist concept of change with a scientific materialist view in an interview with a Galician television station in Spain in 1988. He talked about how the cultural mass process of the revolution deepened understanding about same-sex love.

"God needed seven days to make the world," he said, "you must understand that to remake this world, to destroy a world like that which we had here and to make a new one, there wasn't much light, and at first there was a lot of darkness, and a lot of confusion about a series of problems. Our society, our party, our government now have ideas that are clearer, wiser and more intelligent about many of these problems. Given that we can make mistakes, we obsessively follow the idea of what is just, right and best for the people, and what is the most humane for our people and our society. However, the task is not easy. I think that each time we get closer to the right criteria for making the world we want."

Revolution: 'school of unfettered thought'

Fidel Castro said in a now-famous 1962 talk that the "Revolution must be a school of unfettered thought."

The intellectual and cultural dynamism of the Cuban Revolution, which combined communist leadership with mass participation, is evident in the trajectory of progress in the 1970s made concerning women and same-sex love.

The Cuban leaders continued to organize mass forums for discussion and debate that empowered changes concerning sexuality, sex and gendered social roles.

Two years after the 1971 congress declaration that no homosexual should officially represent the country, it was overruled by a Cuban court. (Hatch)

In 1975, the limits on employment of homosexuals in the arts and education were overturned by the Cuban Supreme Court, which ruled in favor of gay artists who were petitioning for compensation and reinstatement in their workplace. (cuba-solidarity.org.uk)

That same year, a revolutionary Family Code was adopted that called for equal participation by men in child-raising and household work.

Also in 1975, a new Ministry of Culture was established, as well as a commission to study homosexuality.

That commission helped pave the road for the formal decriminalization of same-sex love.

But U.S. imperialism, which had economically exploited the homosexual/transgender population of Cuba before the revolution, continued to exploit them politically. ▼

Behind the 1980 'Mariel boatlift'

Several thousand self-identified homosexual Cubans were among the some 120,000 who left the island over a two-month period in 1980 from the port of Mariel and sailed to the U.S. The media in the imperialist countries, whose capitalist classes were hell-bent on re-colonizing Cuba, broadcast an anti-communist interpretation of what produced that migration at Mariel.

Workers World Party founder Sam Marcy wrote, "The 1970s were the high point in Cuba's revolutionary influence, not only in Latin America but in Africa, Asia and even Europe. Cuba was part of a worldwide surge in the working-class movement and particularly among oppressed countries. U.S. imperialism was on the defensive, especially after its historic defeat in Vietnam and its inability to either crush or tame the Cuban Revolution." (Marcy)

Cuban women and men were fighting bravely alongside their African comrades to defend the people of Angola, Namibia and Ethiopia from colonialism and imperialism.

U.S. finance capital tried to isolate and destroy the Cuban Revolution.

U.S. banks and corporations commanded Washington not to recognize Cuba's right to diplomatic recognition. Captains of the military-industrial complex ordered their generals and admirals to attack the island using various weapons—covert and overt—including enforcement of the economic blockade of the island, which is an illegal act of war. The Pentagon refused to retreat from the military base it built at Guantánamo—now a site where the interrogators incorporate anti-gay and anti-trans humiliation, rape and attempted dehumanization as part of their sadistic torture of Muslim men and boys.

And 1980 was the year that Ronald Reagan won the White House.

Marcy concluded, "A period began when the most intense economic, political and diplomatic pressure was exerted on Cuba. In the background was always the threat of U.S. military intervention, causing the Cuban government to spend a great deal of its resources on military defense."

CIA targeted homosexual Cubans

Between 1979 and 1984—before and after Mariel—scholars Lourdes Arguelles and B. Ruby Rich interviewed Cuban émigrés in the U.S., Spain, Mexico and Puerto Rico. The two researchers also interviewed Cubans who chose to stay on the island and be a part of building a socialist society.

Arguelles and Rich revealed how U.S. finance capital used its secret CIA police agency to politically target the same Cuban homosexual/transgender population it had once exploited for profit.

"The year 1979 was an unsettled one," Arguelles and Rich wrote. "Even though living conditions were better than in any previous period and compared favorably with those in the rest of the Caribbean, there were serious problems." They pointed out that the economy suffered under the heavy weight of the U.S. blockade and suspicious outbreaks of biological epidemics destroyed harvests of cash crops. This forced Cubans to work harder and faster and for longer hours in order to raise overall productivity.

The U.S. allowed Cubans who had emigrated in the early years of the revolution to travel back to the island. Arguelles and Rich noted, "The visits of 'the American cousins' increased consumer envy and added to the effectiveness of counter-revolutionary propaganda.

"Lesbians and gay men were particularly vulnerable," they explained. "The CIA targeted the homosexual intelligentsia and worked to persuade its members to defect, promising generous academic grants and publishing contracts."

Arguelles and Rich continued, "The more cost-effective ploy of blackmail was also used, especially against those gays less willing to leave, in the hope that political anxiety would force victims into exile. Carlos Alberto Montaner, a Madrid-based anti-Castro writer, for example, published two full pages listing names of homosexuals inside Cuba in an attempt to discredit them and to encourage them to migrate. Such cynical 'assistance' in coming out continues to be a favored weapon against lesbians and gay men who are well integrated into the revolution."

The two researchers added, "The visits also provided a context in which Cuban lesbians and gay men could hear of the more open and affluent gay lifestyles available in the United States as a benefit of consumer capitalism. Other common reasons for wanting to emigrate included the lack of career mobility in a still under-developed economy and, for men, a traditional desire for the adventure of travel that had to focus on emigration since the United States and other capitalist nations deny tourist visas to Cubans. For some Cuban gays (especially for the men), emigration also provided wider sexual parameters than they felt could ever be possible in Cuba."

Exception to a rotten rule

U.S. imperialism demonstrated how its laws either kneel to its overall capitalist class objectives, or are forced to bend.

After the Cuban Revolution shut down U.S. finance capital's burgeoning sex and casino industries that had exploited mass numbers of homosexuals, U.S. immigration authorities unofficially lifted the part of the Immigration and Naturalization Act of 1952 that had been used to bar and deport those it labeled "sexually deviant"—but only for homosexual Cubans.

Washington lured Cubans to risk their lives at sea by creating an exception to immigration rules and quotas that barred legal migration to the U.S. Any Cuban who arrived on U.S. soil was promised admission, with perks.

Cuban President Fidel Castro challenged Washington's immigration manipulation and hypocrisy by opening the port at Mariel from April 21 to Sept. 28 in 1980, allowing any Cubans who wanted to leave to go to the U.S. Some 120,000 Cubans left, out of the country's total population of 11 million.

Even the estimates of how many homosexual Cubans left from Mariel in 1980 demonstrate political manipulation by the U.S. government.

Reporting for the publication *Paris Match*, Nina Sutton cited a "nonofficial State Department source" as saying at least 10,000 Cuban homosexuals had emigrated at Mariel. However, Julia Preston stated in the New York *Village Voice* dated Dec. 10-16, 1980, that "As many as 3,000 gay Cubans passed through refugee camps this summer. Now about 350 are left, almost all men, the others having been sponsored out mainly to gay communities throughout the country."

Gay Cubans were not welcomed into the homosexual-hating, right-wing-dominated Cuban émigré enclaves and anti-communist organizations.

Under state duress

At U.S. borders, all individual immigrants face tremendous pressure under interrogation from border police, immigration judges and officials and in detention centers.

Arguelles and Rich explained in 1984 that "Cuban 'refugee' testimony and subsequent conversations with the newly arrived Cubans, for example, becomes the main source for evaluation of Cuban gay life, despite knowledge of the pressures on émigrés to testify to political persecution in their country of origin in order to attain the legal and economic advantages of refugee status in their new country."

Arguelles and Rich stated, "The success of this interpretation has served anti-Cuban interests, most notably the American state, rather well. First, credibility of the story has neutralized badly needed support for the Cuban revolution among its natural allies (North American progressive lobbies) and legitimated the presence in traditionally liberal circles of some of the more reactionary elements within the Cuban émigré population." ▼

'A visible feature of Cuban society'

The thunderous, monopolized voice of the U.S. media machine dwelled on homosexuals who left Cuba from the port of Mariel in 1980, omitting the role of the CIA in instigating migration. At the same time, the U.S.-led political blockade of Cuba silenced the voices of Cubans who chose to stay, working together to actively defend their workers' state against the most powerful imperialist empire in history.

Arguelles and Rich stated, with the clarity of courage, "For all the gay men and the few lesbians who left, there were many more who chose to stay. Their lives had been constantly improving. The revolution might not yet speak to the homosexual in them, but it continued to address other vital aspects of their being." These Cubans, they reported, "steadfastly refused to fulfill their gay identity at the cost of their national and political identities."

Few lesbians left from Mariel, Arguelles and Rich found. "Their small number by comparison with that of gay men points, again, to the fuller integration of women into Cuban society and the increased status and freedom enjoyed by lesbians, as women, under the revolution."

Ada, a lesbian Cuban rural nurse, said that everything in Cuba wasn't "perfect." But, she said, "I remember how it was before [the revolution] and for the first time, I feel I'm a human being.'" (Arguelles)

Arguelles and Rich reported that in this period of their research—1979 to 1984—the homosexual population was "a visible feature of the Cuban social landscape"—part of every sphere of economic, social and governmental organization, as well as at the point of production of art and other forms of culture.

Arguelles and Rich observed, "They are no longer confined to an underworld economy or alienated from the mainstream of social life as they were in the pre-revolutionary era. Particular individuals are well known and pointed to with pride as evidence of revolutionary non-discrimination."

They reported finding "a flourishing homosexual social scene centered around private parties and particular homes." They described this social networking at parties and beaches as "a feature of Havana life in general."

Arguelles and Rich added, "While their sexuality may be an open secret inside Cuba, many lesbians and gay males who participate in cultural and academic exchanges with the

United States become more guarded when abroad, fearful of how homosexual issues are utilized in the war against the Cuban revolution.

"But many still take the opportunity to visit lesbian and gay bars and bath houses in New York or San Francisco," Arguelles and Rich pointed out in the mid-1980s. "Ironically, their own adjustment to a greater social integration in Cuba causes them increasingly to feel out of place in these sites, viewing their sexual consumerism as bizarre."

Jorge, a Cuban artist, concluded that "there is more true sexuality for gays in Cuba." (Arguelles and Rich)

Arguelles and Rich returned to the island after their research had been published in Spanish in the Mexican newspaper *La Jornada*. The response they got from lesbian and gay Cubans was that "Overwhelmingly, they felt that progress was more marked than we suggested and that conditions of daily life had significantly improved during this decade."

A gay Cuban named Roberto who said he had left from Mariel "for the adventure" went back to Cuba to visit. Roberto's experiences in the U.S. drew him to the Antonio Maceo Brigade—pro-revolutionary Cubans in Miami and New Jersey. (Hillson)

When Roberto returned to the island, he visited the factory in which he used to work. His co-workers had known he was homosexual. As Roberto got up to speak to an assembly of 700 of his former factory co-workers, they all rose to give him a standing ovation.

Lift the blockade!

Cubans who are homosexual, transgender and transsexual did not need imperialism to "liberate" them from their own people, their own revolution. They needed and deserved support from the revolutionary and progressive movements in the U.S.—the citadel of anti-Cuban finance capital—and around the world to help defeat imperialism.

Cubans of all sexualities, genders and sexes were suffering, and are still suffering, under the economic warfare of the U.S. blockade.

In addition, the blockade impacted on sexual and gender expression on the island. For example, it put enormous strain on housing, which in turn determines literally how much room and privacy people have to explore their sexual curiosity and desire.

The constant state of military alert demanded a mass mobilization of Cuban women, as well as men, in a collective effort for national defense. Revolutionary military preparedness values courage and strength, dignity and discipline. For half a millennium, colonialism and imperialism had extolled these virtues as birth traits of masculine males.

Colonial ideology, backed up by the ruling church and state, enforced masculine gender expression in males. The Spanish military and church introduced anti-homosexual epithets that seared like branding irons, as its state cruelly punished same-sex love and gender variance.

The most common slur hurled at male homosexuals, which has endured from the medieval Inquisition in Europe, translates into English as "stick of wood." It refers to the feudal European punishment of burning alive at the stake males who had sex with other males, or those deemed inappropriately gendered. Colonialism brought the fire of the Inquisition with its armadas. In the mid-1600s, for example, the Spanish captain general who ruled over the rural and urban enslaved population of Cuba sentenced 20 "effeminate sodomites" to be burned alive.

The anti-gay epithet—hurled at those not considered "manly" enough—has another meaning: coward. It's an accusation faced by those who fled Cuba in the Mariel boatlift.

However, the idea that femininity is "weak" or "cowardly" is a gender prejudice that all feminine people—male-bodied, female-bodied or intersexual—have a common interest in debunking. Feminine Cuban women, for example, have played a heroic role in the revolution—militarily as well as politically

Cuban community defense and military ranks, however, were organizing and mobilizing the entire population as a popular army to defend the collective gains of the Cuban Revolution, not inculcating the kind of Rambo-masculinity indoctrination that the Pentagon drills into its ranks of the foot soldiers of an imperialist empire. Cuba's foreign policy, by contrast, was the export of revolutionary solidarity. ▼

Sex education campaign battled old prejudices

Eva Bjorklund wrote in *Swedish-Cuba* magazine in 2000: "In 1977, the Center for Sexual Education (CNES) [later CENESEX] was founded on the initiative of the Cuban Women's Federation (FMC) and their seminars and publications encouraged a more enlightened outlook on homosexuality and started to undermine traditional prejudices and taboos. The work done by this center has contributed to changes in attitudes and laws, and the credit for the fact that the AIDS problem has not been handled with a homophobic outlook is largely attributed to this endeavor." (Bjorklund)

Bjorklund noted: "Before the Center for Sexual Education (CNES) started its work, sexual education was a practically unknown phenomenon in Cuba, as in the rest of Latin America, where the stand and the attitude of the Catholic Church has continued to curb any attempted change. In this light, Cuba's sexual education is groundbreaking."

Cuban women led the way forward.

Dr. Celestino Álvarez Lajonchere, then-director of the National Institute of Sex Education in Havana, recalled in a 1986 interview: "In 1974, the Federation of Cuban Women has already insisted that sex education had to be done. They had been working on this since the early 1960s." (Fee)

The interview with Álvarez—known on the island as "Tino"—was conducted with Elizabeth Fee, Joan Furman-Seaborg and Ross Conner. Margaret Gilpin arranged the interview and did the translation.

In the interview, Álvarez stressed: "The First Party Congress reviewed all of the things that the Federation has asked for and converted them into a political directive. This is the only country in the world where the people who have suffered from the consequences of ignorance, principally women and young people, did not have to spend one minute to convince the highest levels of leadership of the country that something had to be done. On the contrary, the political leadership was always worried that they weren't doing enough of what the women expected them to do. I am convinced that that doesn't happen in any other country in the world. I think that's important—very important."

Álvarez continued: "The First Party Congress of 1975 agreed on the declaration of the complete and absolute equality of women. The elaboration of that declaration included the need to organize a system of sex education. They needed a plan to create, for example, illustrated texts, and educational materials for the population. The National Assembly of People's Power then created a permanent commission. Within that commission they created a working group, the National Institute of Sex Education. The structure is very important. I don't think that in any country in the world, including the socialist world, does this kind of structure exist, except here."

He added, "With this kind of task, to create a national plan, you can't leave it in the hands of one person or a group of people or to one organization; it has to be done throughout the entire society."

One of the first suggestions the Ministry of Education made was to begin elementary sex education from the earliest years. But Cuba was still trying to build enough schools and train enough teachers to meet the educational needs of the population. Álvarez said his youngest child's teachers at that time in secondary school in the countryside were just two or three years older than their students.

"It was difficult for the Ministry of Education under these circumstances," he stated, "to assume responsibility for a national program in sex education.

"The first task was to prepare some texts on the subject, because there weren't any."

Ground-breaking first publication

Álvarez explained, "We decided to make a selection from the most highly developed socialist country in this area, East Germany, and we selected the books that we thought would best cover our needs."

The first ground-breaking publication in Cuba was Sigfried Schnabl's "The Intimate Life of Males and Females" (El hombre y la mujer en la intimidad). The book had been published first in the German Democratic Republic—the East German workers' state—in 1978.

Bjorklund wrote that Sigfried Schnabl's book, which was "translated and edited in Cuba in 1979, clearly states that 'homosexuals should be granted equal rights, respect and recognition, and that any kind of social discrimination is reprehensible.' This book served as guidance for the work of CNES and at pedagogical colleges."

In their article in the Summer 1980 Gay Insurgent, Stephen J. Risch and Randolph E. Wills noted, "In fact it was the Women's Federation which saw the book as so important that it successfully lobbied for its publication considerably ahead of schedule (since there are limited resources for publishing books in Cuba, finished manuscripts must wait in line to be published)."

Álvarez remembers that the subject was so popular: "We sold it in a special way to try and guarantee that it would get into the hands of doctors, other health personnel and teachers. We sold it at about 5 pesos, but in addition, the buyer had to have a paper signed by me saying that he or she had the right to buy the book. Otherwise, the books would have disappeared from the bookstores within two hours."

The law against same-sex love was removed the same year that the book was published in 1979—almost a quarter century before the U.S. government followed suit under pressure from a mass lesbian, gay, bisexual and trans movement.

A subsequent publication, "Are You Beginning to Think about Love?" translated and edited in Cuba in 1981, "was more ambivalent," wrote Bjorklund. "It was intended for a broad audience and argued that homosexuals have the same ability to function in society as other people, but that they can never be as happy as married people. Mónika Krause, a leading expert at CNES, admitted that this was a response to criticism against the first edition of Schnabl's book, for being too positive towards homosexuality. A second edition of Schnabl's book, intended to be printed in 250,000 copies, although delayed because of the economic crisis, however, persisted, stressing that sexual violation of minors has no causal relationship to sexual orientation, dismissing the theories of seduction into homosexuality, and emphasizing that since nobody is responsible for his or her sexual orientation, homosexuals must be just as respected as heterosexuals."

Álvarez said the next step in sex education was a paperback entitled "When Your Child Asks You" (*Cuando tu hijo te pregunta*), first printed in 1980. It was offered for public sale with a book aimed at sex education for children aged 9 to 12. "We did simple illustrations showing the process of reproduction. This was the best way to start trying to break the prejudices of the population," he stated. "We were trying to tell parents that they didn't have any alternative, they had to tell children about these things, because their kids were going to deal with them for better or for worse. It was up to the parents to answer their kids' questions and they needed to know how to do that."

A fourth publication, "Thinking About Love?" (*¿Piensas ya en el amor?*), was designed for teenagers. Álvarez explained: "This book covers sexually transmitted diseases and discusses some of the emotional aspects of how children become adults and what adult relations are all about. It deals with some of the problems that have to do with being in love, and also talks about contraception."

Yet another book was written for children from 3 to 7 years old, entitled "Mama, Papa and Me" (*Mamá, papá, y yo*). Álvarez said, "It was the only one that didn't sell out immediately, the way all the rest of them did, and we think that's a sign of some resistance to our work in the population."

In 1981, the Cuban Ministry of Culture produced a publication titled "In Defense of Love" that stated homosexuality was a variant of human sexuality. Cuba-solidarity.org.uk concluded that the book "argued that homophobic bigotry was an unacceptable attitude inherited by the Revolution and that all sanctions against gays should be opposed."

This ground-breaking work on sex education, in which Cuban women played such a leadership role, helped pave the road for a scientific and humane approach to the AIDS epidemic that put the imperialist countries to shame. ▼

Cuba mobilized before first diagnosis

▼ The Reagan administration tried to whip up world anger at Cuba's handling of the AIDS epidemic. In reality, Cuba took an immediate, scientific and humane approach to people with AIDS.

In the U.S., AIDS was first diagnosed in 1981. By May 2, 1983, simultaneous gay and lesbian protests of tens of thousands had to take to the streets in New York City, San Francisco, Los Angeles, Houston, Atlanta, Chicago and Milwaukee under banners reading "Fighting for our lives!" to demand federal funds to battle AIDS, and for research, services and Social Security benefits.

A day later, activists organized a telephone blitz of the White House to protest government inaction and to demand funds. It was the largest number of calls to the Oval Office in a single day in its history. The president had still not publicly said the word AIDS, while theo-cons demonized the emerging health crisis as a "gay plague."

By contrast, Cuba's health care workers began preparations to defend the whole population from the AIDS epidemic two years before the first case was diagnosed on the island in 1985. Cuba spared no expense despite the chokehold of the U.S.-led blockade.

Cuba—unlike the U.S.—mobilized against AIDS, not against people with AIDS. Arguelles and Rich observed in the autumn of 1987 that, "Cuba is unusual in publicizing the disease, not as a gay disease, but rather as a sexually transmitted disease regardless of specific sexual practice."

Planning to protect population

After members of the Cuban Health Ministry took part in a workshop organized by the Pan-American Health Organization in August 1983, they immediately set up a national commission to research and create a plan of action to prevent AIDS in Cuba. (Wald)

The commission immediately blocked the import of all blood products from countries in which the epidemic was already documented. The commission recommended discarding more than 20,000 vials of imported blood, worth millions of dollars.

Getting rid of all imported blood products greatly burdened the Cuban health system and forced the country to ratchet up local production. However, this urgent action resulted in avoiding HIV transmission to almost all hemophiliacs and others who needed blood transfusions. (Cookson)

A multi-disciplinary team of doctors and researchers was assigned to work full time on AIDS. Political journalist Karen Wald wrote, "Their first move was to prepare a diagnostic screening program based on concrete symptoms that could be seen in hospitals, such as repeated cases of pneumonia or Kaposi's sarcoma type of cancer, which indicated possible AIDS. Hospitals were asked to give weekly reports on findings of these symptoms."

Doctors tested more than 135,000 Cubans for HIV in 1983.

Science, not stigma

In 1985, a Cuban who had returned from abroad was the first in the country to be diagnosed with AIDS. The Cuban was one of 300,000 heroes of the revolution who helped defend the people of Mozambique—an African country impoverished by colonialism and battling the forces of imperialism.

In the U.S., Africa and Haiti were being scapegoated as the source of the epidemic, without any scientific proof. In Cuba, however, where many are of African descent because of the history of slavery, health officials did not stigmatize the African continent.

In an interview in *Cuba International*, circa 1987, Dr. Rodolfo Rodríguez, then the national director of epidemiology for the Cuban Ministry of Health, said that while some of the mass media at that time might have been trying to blame the African continent for AIDS, "It is known worldwide that it is the developed Western countries—Europe and the U.S.—that have the largest number of AIDS cases and the largest number of asymptomatic carriers."

In the U.S., homosexuality was still against the law and viciously repressed. The right wing labeled AIDS a "gay disease." This only drove the epidemic deeper into the population. So too did the criminalization of drug addiction and prostitution, both highly profitable industries in the U.S.

Neither friend nor foe of the Cuban Revolution has ever reported any indication of the social crisis of intravenous drug use on the island. And same-sex love was not against the law in Cuba.

Cuban health workers tested all pregnant women, people with sexually transmitted diseases, and anyone who might have had sexual contact with someone who was HIV positive. Testing equipment was installed in blood bank centers. (Aguilera)

By the end of 1985, Wald wrote, the Cuban government had purchased, despite great expense, all the technical means to screen the island's entire blood supply. "Cuba spent more than $3 million to buy the reactive agents and equipment, and to set up labs in blood banks and hygiene and epidemiology centers around the country."

That year, the Cuban public health system allocated $2 million for the National HIV/AIDS Prevention and Control Program, which focused on providing the first 750,000 diagnostic kits and centers. (Editors: "Cuba's HIV-AIDS Rate")

Capitalism and contraception

The years of sex education that preceded the outbreak of the epidemic helped to create the basis for a more scientific and compassionate approach to people with AIDS.

However, when faced with a sexually transmissible epidemic like AIDS, Cuba had to overcome a particular capitalist legacy regarding safer-sex education and practices.

Dr. Celestino Álvarez Lajonchere, a gynecologist and ground-breaking sex educator in Cuba, reminded interviewers in 1988, "You know this country inherited a system in which the rural areas and small towns had little or no medical care before the revolution." (Fee)

He added that before the revolution, illegal abortions were common. They were most often performed by doctors, without anesthesia, in unsanitary conditions.

Álvarez Lajonchere explained: "At the triumph of the revolution, the majority of these abortion doctors left the country. There was no habit in the country of using contraceptives, and contraception did not even appear in the medical school curriculum. … The private physicians at the time didn't give contraceptive services to their patients because they could charge much more doing abortions."

As a result, he said, "Since people didn't have contraceptive habits, we encountered serious difficulties in the first years after the triumph of the revolution."

While half of all Cuban doctors left the island and went to capitalist countries, 97 percent of the physicians in obstetrics and gynecology emigrated. As a result, Álvarez Lajonchere noted, overnight he became the oldest gynecologist/obstetrician in the country.

Álvarez Lajonchere said that, in addition, within months after the workers and peasants took state power, "[A]ll of the professors at the medical school quit voluntarily, thinking mistakenly that the government could not replace them. The government accepted their resignations. It was a policy in the country, and still is, that if you really don't want to live in this country under socialism you should leave. You can't create a socialist society with people who are disaffected.

"So the Ministry of Education and the Ministry of Public Health got together a course for new professors," he continued, "people who could never have been professors before the revolution because of their low social class origins—they didn't come from the upper middle classes."

The medical school faculty was replaced with new professors. "We all left private practice and went to teach. It was an extraordinary advantage that we knew the conditions of medical practice in the country. I became chief of the department of obstetrics and gynecology at the one and only medical school. The first thing I did was to put contraception into the medical school curriculum. There were never any restrictions about who could have access to contraceptives in this country: not by age, not by race, not by anything."

Álvarez Lajonchere added, "Medical services from the very beginning have been free." And the new medical teachers received a higher salary than the president. (Fee)

"The habit of using contraceptives," Álvarez Lajonchere explained, "is a habit that takes time to build. For a population that was accustomed to having abortions, it was easier for them to go to the hospital and have an abortion."

After the revolution, underground abortions in unsanitary conditions increased until 1965. "When we started to do all of them in hospitals, obviously deaths as a result of abortion disappeared."

He added that the number of abortions began to decrease in 1974 as a result of mass education about sex and contraception.

Álvarez Lajonchere concluded: "Our current policy on population is the same policy that we've had from the first day of the revolution. It's a policy of principle. A woman has the right to have the number of children she wants, and to have them when she wants. The government is obligated to assure that her right becomes a reality. So we educate people about all of the contraceptive methods. We include abortion, even though we don't view it as a contraceptive method, so that people will know about it. We have never said that having a small family is good; we have never pressured people to reduce the birth rate." ▼

Care & prevention, not repression

From both a scientific and human standpoint, the AIDS sanatoria health care facilities in Cuba bore no relation to the threat of state quarantine in the U.S.

In the U.S., there was no scientific merit to public proposals to empower the state for surveillance and quarantine of people believed to have AIDS. There was no way to identify how many people out of the vast population had already been exposed. The epidemic was already entrenched by the mid-1980s. AIDS was not spread through casual contact. And anti-gay and racist scapegoating, laws against same-sex love, immigrant bashing, and laws against IV drug use and prostitution had generated fear of the state, as well as of coming forward for testing or treatment. The prohibitive costs of medical care, particularly for those without health insurance, also barred many from seeking health care.

So threats of state investigation and forced isolation only drove the epidemic deeper underground. Yet on March 2, 1984, *USA Today* revealed that California officials were legally pursuing the ability to forcibly quarantine people believed to have AIDS. The same month, the Democratic co-chair of the Connecticut General Assembly's Judiciary Committee introduced broad quarantine legislation after a racist media campaign demonized a Black woman, accused of prostitution and drug addiction, who was reported to have AIDS.

Even as politicians were refusing to allocate the funds necessary to meet the AIDS public health emergency, the racist big-business media were accusing Haitian immigrants in the U.S. of spreading AIDS.

The late AIDS activist Michael Callen told *Workers World* at that time that the press for quarantine powers was "not really to protect people but to further certain political goals, to further isolate already disenfranchised people." Callen said that the singling out of a Black woman in Connecticut and allegations without scientific basis that Haiti and Africa were the sources of the epidemic were attempts "to blame all calamity on the Third World." (Feinberg, "The government didn't care")

Gay men and bisexuals were blamed for the epidemic for much the same reason that the church hierarchy in the Middle Ages accused Jewish people of creating bubonic plague by "poisoning the wells."

Media in the South and Jerry Falwell's right-wing fundamentalist publication *Moral Majority Inc.* editorialized that AIDS was God's "deserved punishments" against homosexuals. (aidssurvivalproject.org)

Far-right columnist Patrick Buchanan titled his commentary: "AIDS Disease: It's Nature Striking Back."

That's why the late Bobbi Campbell, a San Francisco registered nurse with AIDS, told *Workers World* in 1984 how concerned he was about the political abuses of broad quarantine measures in the U.S. He warned, "We would see gay men locked up en masse and it is possible in more backward localities that lesbians could be included in that." ("Bobbi Campbell calls for solidarity")

The U.S. government declared war on people with AIDS rather than marshal funds and forces to deal with the epidemic.

Science, not scapegoating

By contrast, Cuba—an island nation of 11 million that was blockaded by U.S. imperialism—had prepared its health care system for the epidemic two years before its first diagnosis of an AIDS case. So when AIDS first emerged in the population, it could be easily identified and isolated before being spread to the rest of the people.

In 1986, Cuba opened up 13 sanatoria that provided care for 99 people, only 20 percent of whom were believed to have contracted AIDS through same-sex contact. (Aguilera)

Joseph Mutti wrote from Havana in June 1999, "Once a person has tested HIV-positive, attempts are made to trace everyone who had sexual contact with the person. Given Cubans' general openness about their sexuality, and Cuba's cradle-to-grave health care system, it's usually possible to ascertain how and when a person was infected.

"The basic principle of the Cuban public health-care system, widely recognized as the Third World's best," Mutti explained, "is to prioritize the health of the population as a whole instead of focusing exclusively on individual care. This is important for understanding HIV/AIDS policies, including the sanatorium system that earned Cuba an unfair reputation for employing repression to counter the virus." (Mutti)

The newspaper *Granma* explained Cuba's reasons for using quarantine: "The main usefulness of this measure is to slow down as much as possible the epidemic progression of the disease to allow time for other measures of disease control to have a medium- or long-term effect, such as education (encouraging changes in sexual habits and behavior), until such time as a vaccine and treatment exist, auguring a definitive solution to the problem." ("Cuban Strategy")

When asked about the Cuban approach to AIDS, then-Cuban Deputy Public Health Minister Hector Terry explained in October 1987, "The quarantine center is a sanatorium. We have a very small number of people carrying the virus, and we believe that because of that, we are in a unique situation. We have an opportunity, in epidemiological terms, of controlling the spread of AIDS and preventing it from becoming a major

Left to right: The late Michael Callen, Leslie Feinberg, and the late Bobbi Campbell at first national AIDS protest march in Washington, D.C., Oct. 8, 1983.

epidemic as it has in other countries, where they don't know how to confront, reduce or eliminate it.

"We are in a situation that permits us to make this kind of decision, and to wait a while because we are not talking about something permanent, for a whole lifetime. We're talking about a dialectical situation."

Terry added, "This aspect [quarantine] is controversial, some groups of scientists disagree with it." He said that the objections were "more from a political than a scientific standpoint. But we believe our country has this epidemiological opportunity and we shouldn't lose it. We are trying to prevent the spread of the virus throughout the country by means of sexual relations that our patients could have with other people who at this point have not been infected with the virus.

"Our country has its own philosophy and the first principle of this philosophy is respect for human dignity. I think that human dignity requires care of the individual. You know that we spare no resources here to make sure that our people have the best health care possible anywhere in the world. And that's part of what we're trying to maintain in our battle against AIDS." (Wald, 1987)

The best care—for free

Cuba provided free health care to its population despite economic obstruction by the U.S. and later the devastating loss of its main trading partner, the Soviet Union. Cuba organized its scarce resources—not just to stem transmission of the epidemic, but to provide humane care.

"Organized like small communities," *MEDICC Review* editors wrote in 2001, "the sanatoriums are made up of apartment complexes and small houses, plus infirmary, offices and other patient facilities." ("Cuba's HIV-AIDS Rate")

People with AIDS received healthy food, medications and other treatment, air-conditioned housing, exercise and sports, movies, television, videos, rest, and psychological and social services; everything was free except cigarettes.

Cubans with AIDS continued to receive their full paychecks, even if they weren't able to work. Their jobs were held open indefinitely. Terry stressed, "This is very important, so that they have no concern regarding the support of their families.

"What other country in the world would be capable of paying full salary to people with AIDS?" Terry asked. "I think that's very linked to the whole question of human rights and the controversies around this. We know there are countries that shout about human rights, such as the U.S. where a person who gets AIDS may die of hunger, lose his job, it's hard to get into a hospital. Treatment there costs an average of $700 a day."

Terry added that the Cubans' families also received special attention. A working group of psychologists, sociologists and social workers helped the families of people with AIDS deal with their problems, as well. Terry concluded that people with AIDS had greater peace of mind knowing their families were being cared for. ▼

Cuba brought science, not scapegoating, to AIDS care

Cuba tried to isolate the spread of AIDS as soon as the epidemic appeared in the island population, explained then-Cuban Deputy Public Health Minister Hector Terry in 1987. But Cuba did not try to socially isolate people with AIDS.

Terry stressed of Cubans living in the sanatoria, "They visit their families at home, go out on pass; their families visit them, every day. Their friends can visit them." (Wald)

Cuba attempted to quarantine the spread of the epidemic based on a scientific approach to a medical emergency, without using scapegoating to isolate people with AIDS.

In the U.S., AIDS activists had to fight a protracted battle to replace the bigoted label of "high-risk groups" with a rational understanding of "high-risk behaviors." Cuban medical workers and educators approached transmission scientifically.

Arguelles and Rich observed in the autumn of 1987 that, "Cuba is unusual in publicizing the disease, not as a gay disease, but rather as a sexually transmitted disease regardless of specific sexual practice."

The primary route of AIDS transmission in Cuba was via international contact, including Cubans who had worked or studied abroad.

Of the first 99 people quarantined in 1986, only about 20 percent were believed to have contracted AIDS through same-sex contact.

Terry articulated this clearly: "We are carrying out our program by giving the public a lot of scientific information, speaking to them clearly about the modes of transmission and not generating phenomena such as homophobia or sexual repression.

"In some countries the mass media, for commercial reasons, generate those phenomena to sell more magazines or newspapers. But we don't need to sell more magazines or newspapers. We don't need to use AIDS to get people to watch more TV or to get some corporation to finance AIDS research. We don't need any of that here."

Terry summed up, "We start from the ideas that AIDS is transmitted not because of what you are but because of what you do, and therefore there's no reason to generate any kind of persecution or phobia against any patient."

Interviewer Karen Wald added, "Members of the gay community interviewed here said there has been no increase in homophobia or attacks on gays as a result of AIDS.

They attribute this in part to the fact that the government has not singled out gays as carriers of the disease."

Eyewitness to Cuban care

Cleo Manago was part of a delegation of 200 people from the U.S. who challenged Washington's travel ban to visit Cuba in August 1994. Manago wrote about his visit to an AIDS sanatorium in an article entitled "Cuba, from a Black, Male, Same-Gender-Loving Perspective."

"The widely reported rumors and articles on AIDS concentration camps in Cuba are out of context and pure anti-Cuba propaganda," Manago stated. "I visited Cuba's largest AIDS sanatorium and was taken aback by the humane, considerate, intuitive and life affirming approach to care taken by this center.

"The sanatorium was similar to a large housing complex where all who chose to live there had 24-hour health care, the option of having family members, even a dog or a cat stay with them. Same-gender-loving and heterosexual couples living together at the complex is a common occurrence.

"I asked people living there about the conditions in which they live. None were happy about having HIV or AIDS but all were very appreciative of the care they received. Many who could go home if they wanted chose to stay where they were guaranteed prepared food, a comfortable home and prompt medical attention. This particular center offered ambulatory care for those with jobs or who wanted to continue with school. To my knowledge there is nothing similar in the U.S.A."

Manago concluded, "The main problem people with AIDS faced was the difficulty in getting the medicines and treatments (pentamidine, bactrim, condoms, etc.) needed from other countries, due to the U.S. blockade of Cuba." (Manago)

'Information without sensationalism'

Dr. Hector Terry emphasized in 1987, "We are treating the patients medically to maintain their present state of good health. Every time some new information comes up in the scientific community, some new kind of drug or medicine, we try to find out if it could be useful in preventing the virus from becoming activated into a full-blown disease."

Terry added, "Information is reaching the public without any sensationalism, without creating any hysteria or panic. We haven't yet been using the mass media as much as we should; we think that's a deficiency in the program. We've been using state agencies and all the ministries a lot, organizing conferences for all the workers in certain ministries, especially those in the high-risk areas. We also utilize the health education program and the popular video centers throughout the country. We run videos and have doctors there to answer questions. We've used that a lot and many young people attend these.

"We're now preparing other activities with the mass organizations, the Committees to Defend the Revolution, student and women's organizations," he continued. "We are working with other scientific institutions in the country, which are providing invaluable

Billboards aren't used to sell products in Cuba, but to bring important education to all—like this AIDS awareness sign.

assistance and we are looking at all possibilities anywhere in the world. We try to synthesize what is being done internationally.

"Here we have the SUMA group, which is developing Cuban technology to do mass-scale diagnostic testing. With an infinitesimal blood sample we can diagnose for AIDS. We'll be trying to get this equipment into all the country's blood banks next year, and in all the hygiene and epidemiology centers. And we'll be preparing ourselves for carrying out at least annual blood tests of the whole population, in every blood bank and epidemiology center, in every hospital. We're preparing a very wide-range program."

Terry concluded, "I repeat that the method of quarantine in a sanatorium isn't permanent. It will be treated dialectically. We are studying the situation and when we see that it is not the correct solution, or that other possibilities offer themselves, we will act accordingly—always basing ourselves on scientific data. Otherwise we wouldn't be scientists."

Clearly quarantine in Cuba was a tactic at the moment the epidemic emerged, not a scientific principle.

Joseph Mutti wrote from Havana in June 1999, "The government undertook extensive efforts to learn more about transmission of the virus and to discover a cure. It wasn't until the early 1990s that officials felt enough was known to end the quarantine and focus on public information, education and prevention."

Cuba began an out-patient pilot reintegration project in 1993 that proved successful. (Aguilera)

Those who left the sanatoria received ambulatory care that included regular doctor's care, visits to specialists and dietary supplements—all free. (medicc.org)

However, the *Denver Post* concluded in February 2003, "Today, 48 percent of those who are HIV-positive or have AIDS choose to live in the 16 sanatoriums around Cuba." (Aguilera) ▼

U.S. imperialist blockade obstructed Cuban AIDS treatment

The Cuban approach to AIDS saved lives, Joseph Mutti stated in June 1999. "Cuba now has one of the world's lowest rates of infection, with only one of every 1,500 persons testing HIV-positive (the U.S. rate is 1 of every 550). That statistic is especially remarkable given Cuba's sexually active youth and easygoing attitudes about sex."

MEDICC Review editors explained that, "By the end of 2001, Cuba will have approved its most ambitious offensive yet against HIV/AIDS: setting up a National Task Force Against AIDS (GOPELS)," to be headed by the minister of public health and the secretary of the council of ministers.

"Their job will be to integrate prevention strategies among the various national players, including the Public Health and Education Ministries, the Federation of Cuban Women, and other government agencies and NGOs. They will be guided by the 'Strategic Plan for Controlling HIV/AIDS,' outlining national strategies against the virus for the next five years." ("Cuba's Strategy")

The biggest problem in dealing with AIDS on the island continued to be access to medicine for free distribution to the population because of the U.S. blockade.

MEDICC Review noted in 2001 that, "Early treatment of AIDS consisted of AZT, interferons and other drugs commonly used in international protocols—but often more difficult for Cuba to purchase because many were patented by U.S. pharmaceutical companies and therefore not freely available to Cuban importers under the restrictions imposed by the U.S. embargo.

"Earlier this year, Cuba began to manufacture its own anti-retrovirals and make them available to AIDS patients free of charge. Cuba has maintained a strong research component in the fight against AIDS, primarily through studies of the application of interferons to AIDS patients and the continued research to develop an HIV/AIDS vaccine."

In February 2003, treatment of Cubans with AIDS had greatly improved over the past two years because Cuba's pharmaceutical industry was producing its own generic copies of anti-HIV medicines. Dr. Byron Barksdale, director of a U.S. medical group, said, "Cuba now produces enough anti-viral medicines for its own patients and it has offered to supply other nations in the Caribbean region." (Cookson)

The *Financial Times*—no friend to socialist construction—reported, "Cuba has much to teach the world about tackling AIDS, the American Association for the Advancement of Science heard on [Feb. 16, 2003]. A wide-ranging prevention and treatment program, backed by strong political action, has given the Caribbean country the lowest prevalence of AIDS disease and HIV infection in the western hemisphere—and one of the lowest rates in the world." (Cookson)

Cuba addresses world impact

In its issue coinciding with International AIDS Day 2001, *MEDICC* Review noted, "Today, some 36 million people worldwide are infected with HIV, over 25 million of them in Africa, where most have no way to pay for the drugs that might extend their lives. They die with no treatment in sight." ("Cuba's HIV-AIDS Rate")

MEDICC Review reprinted the full text of a speech by Cuban Vice President Carlos Lage Dávila, delivered earlier that year at the United Nations General Assembly on AIDS. Lage Dávila had offered his socialist government's solidarity for people with AIDS, "especially those in the developing countries most affected."

In his speech on June 25, 2001, Lage Dávila said, "No country is free of AIDS. Some—the privileged and rich—have managed to reduce the mortality rate with medicines sold at high, unreasonable prices. Others—unfortunate and poor—are experiencing a terrifying reduction in their population's life expectancy and a demographic decline that could lead them to extinction."

He stressed that, "In many African nations, the number of teachers who die from AIDS each year is greater than the number of new teachers graduating. The deaths in sub-Saharan Africa to date are equivalent to those that would have resulted from dropping on the region 70 bombs like the ones on Hiroshima and Nagasaki. It is a dramatic paradox that, in this new millennium, the same continent that witnessed the appearance of humankind's first ancestors six million years ago begins to witness the disappearance of humankind.

"Cuba also suffers from this disease; there have been 2,565 people living with HIV/AIDS in our country, 388 of whom currently have the full-blown disease, and 896 of whom have died over the last 14 years.

"Our program to fight AIDS," Lage Dávila explained, "guarantees comprehensive care for people with HIV and AIDS, free anti-retroviral treatment for all, specialized medical centers for those who require them and a constant struggle for patients to achieve the fullest social integration, with all their rights and without discrimination.

"It also guarantees access to safe blood, certifying that 100 percent of blood donations are free of AIDS, hepatitis and other illnesses; voluntary testing of all pregnant women, resulting in zero mother-child transmission since 1997; and an education and prevention strategy aimed at vulnerable groups, young people and the entire population. We have the lowest AIDS rate in the Americas and one of the lowest in the world, with 0.3 percent of the population between 15 and 49 years affected.

"Even in the face of the [U.S.] blockade, which prevents our access to 50 percent of the world's new medicines because they are produced in the United States," Lage Dávila stressed, "we have controlled the epidemic, and what is more, achieved a life expectancy of 76 years and an infant mortality rate of less than seven. Cuban participates in this Assembly as a responsible member of the international community, showing solidarity and modesty and freely offering our experience and collaboration."

Solidarity proposal

Lage Dávila stated, "The U.N. Secretary General has proposed—and is making a worthy and just effort to obtain—$7 to $10 billion for the fight against AIDS. The amount is not enough and money alone cannot solve the problem, but it is a necessary start. It is incomprehensible to think that this life-saving money cannot be found in a world that spends 40 times more on illegal drugs, 80 times more on military budgets and 100 times more on advertising.

"It is incomprehensible to think that this life-saving money cannot be found in a world where 20 percent of the population is responsible for 86 percent of private consumption, and where the personal fortunes of 22 people each exceed the amount the Secretary General is requesting, fortunes that in total represent 43 times his request."

Lage Dávila pointed to the U.S.: "The richest and most powerful nation in history—that claims it is a human rights champion, does not make its payments to the U.N. and is trying to reduce its contribution to the WHO [World Health Organization]—dedicates barely 0.2 percent of its gross domestic product to development. It is the only country that voted against the resolution giving every individual the right to have access to AIDS medicines, while at the same time, it has unleashed an insane arms race upon the world, with the sale of the most sophisticated instruments of war to allies and followers, and its global missile shield initiative.

"There is no need to elaborate further to understand that the international economic order is criminally unjust, that when the words 'democracy,' 'human rights,' 'individual liberty,' 'equal opportunities' and others come from the mouths of the powerful, they ring hollow and demagogic."

Lage Dávila delivered Cuba's urging that the special session of the U.N. General Assembly proclaim that:

"AIDS drugs and other vital medicines required on a large scale should not be protected by patents. People cannot be allowed to make money off the lives of human beings.

"The foreign debt of the poorest countries should be cancelled immediately and unconditionally. They have already paid more than once.

"The next Group of Seven meeting, instead of adopting a new economic liberalization to impose on the world's poor and less fortunate, should agree to reduce their military budgets to raise at least U.S. $10 billion requested by the U.N. And they should turn these funds over today, not sit by while 25 million more people die. This is merely a small part of their social debt to the Third World."

Cuban government offer

Lage Dávila concluded with an offer from the Cuban government to the poorest countries and those with the highest prevalence of the illness:

- Four thousand doctors and health personnel to create the necessary infrastructure to supply the population with the prescription drugs and necessary follow-up and to train a large number of specialists in their own fields, including nurses and allied health technicians.

- Sufficient professors to establish 20 medical schools, many of whom could be chosen out of the 2,359 Cuban doctors who were then serving in 17 countries as part of Cuba's Integral Health Program. These schools could train 1,000 doctors annually in countries that need the most assistance.

- Doctors, teachers, psychologists and other specialists needed to assess and collaborate with campaigns to prevent AIDS and other illnesses.

- Diagnostic equipment and kits necessary for basic prevention programs.

- Anti-retroviral treatment for 30,000 patients.

Lage Dávila concluded, "All it would take is for the international community to provide the raw materials for the medicines, the equipment and material resources for these products and services. Cuba would not obtain any profits, and would pay salaries in its national currency, thus taking on the most expensive part for international health agencies, as well as the most difficult part, which is to ensure that the professionals are prepared and ready to begin their work."

The U.S.-led political and economic blockade of Cuba kept this offer of socialist solidarity from reaching those around the world who most needed it. ▼

Change apparent in still photos and motion pictures

In 1987, two years into the AIDS epidemic and on the eve of the overturning of the Soviet Union—Cuba's primary trading partner—and the East European bloc of workers' states, the Cuban Revolution continued to make great gains in the battle against old, obstinate prejudice against same-sex love.

Qualitative developments of great import took place in Cuba in the late 1980s.

Hechavarría and Hatch wrote that in 1987, the police were "forbidden to harass people because of appearance or clothing, largely benefiting gays."

A year later, another important change in Cuban law occurred. Pre-revolutionary legislation against "flaunting homosexuality" in public was rescinded. That edict had threatened feminine males and masculine females of all sexualities since its imposition under U.S. neo-colonial rule in the 1930s.

Punishment for homosexual acts had already been formally removed from Cuban law, back in 1979—almost a quarter of a century before the U.S. decriminalized same-sex love.

Arguelles and Rich noted, though, that the 1979 legal code had "failed to legalize manifestations of homosexual behavior in the public sphere and left intact anti-gay laws dating to the Cuban Social Defense Code of 1939."

Arguelles and Rich, summarizing their research in Cuba in the mid-1980s, made a very important point about the difference between private and public spheres in a society building socialism that might not be readily apparent to anyone living in a capitalist system.

They explained, "As delineated in a Latin American socialist setting, private space is far wider than in the United States, encompassing virtually all behavior outside the purview of official sanction or attention, while approved policy, published texts, and official stances compose the public sphere."

They added that "within the private sphere, there are a clear latitude and range of possibilities for lesbians and gay men that surprise the critical observer."

Canadian activist Ian Lumsden quoted a gay émigré living in Toronto, who stated in regard to gay men that "homosexuals in Cuba find it much easier to be open and free about conveying sexual desire in the street than they would in Canada."

In 1988 Cuba took another major step by striking down the imperialist-era "Public Ostentation Law" against "public scandal" or "extravagance."

Revolutionary leadership, mass participation

Cuban society was not changing in some automatic, unconscious way. These developments—which are both a reflection of the growth of consciousness and an effort to raise wider, deeper consciousness—were the result of revolutionary leadership, with widespread popular discussion and debate.

In 1986, Fidel Castro and the Cuban Communist Party had initiated a popular campaign, "not simply to rectify errors committed in the last 10 years," the Cuban president emphasized, "or errors committed throughout the history of the revolution. Rectification is finding the way to resolve errors that are hundreds of years old." (Hillson)

That same year, Cuba's National Commission on Sex Education stated that homosexuality is a sexual orientation and announced the goal of countering homophobia with education. (From the film "Gay Cuba")

In 1988, Fidel Castro spoke out publicly about the need to change negative attitudes in society and in the party about homosexuality. (Hatch)

At the 1992 congress of the Union of Young Communists, Cuban revolutionary leader Vilma Espín, president of the Federation of Cuban Women (FMC), challenged prejudicial ideas about homosexuality presented by a psychologist. (Hatch)

Sonia de Vries, director of the film "Gay Cuba," reported that Espín stated that what needed changing was prejudice, not gay and lesbian sexuality. (Hillson)

That same year, Fidel Castro stated in an interview: "I am absolutely opposed to any form of repression, contempt, scorn or discrimination with regard to homosexuals. [It is] a natural human tendency that must simply be respected." (Borge)

These qualitative changes in Cuba, like still photographs, capture the peaks of progress.

The release of three films in the 1990s—"Strawberry and Chocolate," "Gay Cuba" and "Butterflies on the Scaffold"—offered a moving picture of the sweep of progress resulting from decades of the process of building socialism despite the imperialist military, economic and political blockade.

From the balcony to the screen

When Havana was ruled by U.S. crime bosses and bankers, capitalism made room in the market for homosexual acts, forced to serve the fantasies of those who could afford the cost in dollars and pesos. Often the elite who paid for sex despised those who they exploited—hating them for their class, their race, their sex and/or their gender expression and for witnessing the cruelty, self-hatred, guilt and shame in patrician desire.

So there were lots of homosexual acts taking place in Havana—the biggest U.S. brothel industry in the Caribbean. But off the clock there was not much social room for two men or two women of any gender expression to meet and get to know each other, to freely follow same-sex attraction and exploration, or to fall in love and/or live together as couples or in other formations.

Many men found each other in the darkened theaters of old Cuban cinemas like the Campoamor, Rialto and Verdun. One older Cuban homosexual recalled, "[Y]ou could go and immediately pick up a young guy. Many had their first experience there. There was a lot of sex in those cinemas." (Lumsden)

The culture of Cuba changed with social ownership of the means of production on the island—the land, mines, factories and other major arteries of economic life.

The Cuban Revolution did not, and could not, wave a magic wand and instantly transform the social content of culture. But it quickly transformed the economic character of culture. Like everything else that is collectively produced on the island, culture began to be produced to meet the social needs of the many, not just packaged for individual consumption for the few.

Lumsden reported the ways in which he saw culture being made available to everyone in Cuba in 1996. "This is evident in the low prices and range of theater, dance and music that are available on stage or in open spaces like the Parque Central in Old Havana. It is evident in the quantity and quality of translated foreign and domestic books that have been published at low prices in huge editions. Finally it is evident in events such as the annual film festival (New Latin American Cinema), which has an impact as great as Toronto's Festival."

Lumsden observed, "When you attend a cultural event in Havana you come away as impressed by the informed and critical engagement of the audience as you are by the innovative quality of the performance itself. This involvement is far removed from the commodified nature of so many mainstream cultural events in North America."

This is the Cuban audience to which the state sponsored the release of the 1993 blockbuster movie "Strawberry and Chocolate." The film, about an attempt at friendship and understanding between a young heterosexual communist and a male homosexual intellectual brought same-sex love out of the cinema balconies, where shame and guilt lurked in the shadows, and onto the silver screen of Cuban culture.

Over the next two years, two important documentaries followed—"Gay Cuba" and "Butterflies on the Scaffold."

All told, these movies offer a view of the influence of revolutionary process on popular culture, as well as the influence of popular culture on revolutionary development. The films are themselves part of that dialectical struggle, which itself takes place within the battle against ruling imperialist ideology, broadcast at every turn by its entertainment, media and education industries. ▼

'Strawberry & Chocolate': the sweet taste of change

In 1993, the Cuban state sponsored a ground-breaking movie, "Strawberry and Chocolate" (Fresa y chocolate).

The movie tells the story of two young Cuban men—a heterosexual communist and a homosexual. In his 1995 Cineaste article, Dennis West described the movie as about two young men getting to know each other in Havana in 1979. David is the young communist. Diego, the homosexual, West writes, "leaves in spite of his pro-Revolution sympathies and his friend's claim that there is a place for gays in the Cuban Revolution." (West)

The release of "Strawberry and Chocolate" in Cuba broke national box office records and opened up an island-wide discussion about same-sex love and prejudice.

The movie's script is an adaptation by author Senel Paz of his own very popular short story, "The Wolf, the Woods and the New Man."

Dennis West interviewed acclaimed Cuban director Tomás Gutiérrez Alea—affectionately known to friends as "Titón" but also referred to as Alea—in August 1994. Gutiérrez died, at age 68, in April 1996. West conducted the interview in Juarez, Mexico, during the Second Festival of Latinamerican Cinema Paso del Norte; Dennis West and Joan M. West translated the interview into English, edited it and published it in the Winter-Spring 1995 edition of *Cineaste*.

The movie, which played simultaneously at 10 to 12 Havana theaters, drew lines of Cubans that stretched for blocks. (Oberg)

When West asked Gutiérrez why he thought his movie "Strawberry and Chocolate" so resonated in Cuba, the filmmaker answered that as soon as the movie opened after the annual film festival, "There were very long lines to see it, and it ran for something like three months in Havana. I think it had that response because it was a well-told story with a theme that many people wanted to discuss in public. A theme that up until this time had remained rather marginalized. I'm not referring just to the theme of homosexuality, but rather to the theme of intolerance in general. I think that people really felt a great need to reflect on this, and to reflect on it openly. For these reasons, the film became a sociological phenomenon."

When asked about the number of Cuban viewers who attended screenings, Gutiérrez said, "'Strawberry and Chocolate' may hold the record for the greatest number of Cuban viewers. I don't know. But at any rate, it is the film which has attracted the greatest number of viewers in the shortest period of time."

Gutiérrez contrasted 1979, the year in which "Strawberry and Chocolate" is set, with life on the island in 1995: "Now there is greater flexibility in job opportunities for homosexuals. In the case of representing Cuba abroad, for example, the appointment of representatives used to be handled with kid gloves when homosexuals were involved. Many people were against appointing them because they were considered more vulnerable to scandal and blackmail—and that's true, we've seen it in countries such as England and the United States—but things are very different nowadays for homosexuals."

Gutiérrez summed up, "Many Cuban homosexuals are now open about their sexual orientation. Others are not open about it—just like anywhere else—but there is a new level of awareness concerning homosexuality."

Gutiérrez recalled the experience of his friend Aramis, who told him in Havana in 1994 about an argument with his father. Aramis said when he returned home for a visit with shoulder-length hair, his father used an anti-gay slur and ordered his son to get a haircut or leave.

Gutiérrez said Aramis argued with his father, saying, "You're supposed to be a communist, for freedom, for human beings. I'm your son, you should love me, whether or not I'm a homosexual. What kind of communist are you?"

Gutiérrez said by the time Aramis had stormed to the door, his father stopped him with these words: "Wait. You're right. You can stay. You don't have to cut your hair. I've got to think about these things." Aramis added, "So we hugged, and I stayed."

'The trajectory of Cuban cinema'

Julia Levin, a Latvian freelance film critic who lives in the U.S., described Gutiérrez Alea as the most famous director in Cuba. She noted that the filmmaker was born to a bourgeois family in 1928. After getting a law degree from the University of Havana, he studied film at "the Centro Sperimentale della Cinematographia in Rome (which had spawned, amongst others, Michelangelo Antonioni), where he fell in love with cinema and where he directed his first neorealist film, El Mégano (1954), with Julio Garcia Espinosa, another filmmaker he met at Centro Sperimentale."

Levin continued, "It has been noted that this film marked the very beginning of the New Latin American Cinema, the 'new wave' in cinema that grew out of the desire by many Latin American filmmakers to unveil the conflicting realities of their own countries and to do this by exploring the political potential of the filmic medium.

"Alea was one of the founders of the Instituto Cubano del Arte y la Industria Cinematográficos (ICAIC)," Levin wrote, "which was created in 1959 in order to vigorously produce and promote cinema as the most progressive vehicle for communicating the ideas of the revolutionary through, for the most part, documentaries, although some fiction films were made there as well.

"The ICAIC recognized film as the most powerful and important art form in modern life, a voice of the state, and, unquestionably, the most accessible form of distributing revolutionary ideas to the masses. In its first 24 years, ICAIC produced nearly 900 documentaries and over 112 feature films."

Levin pointed out, "Artistically and intellectually, the trajectory of Cuban cinema—from cinéma vérité to experimentalism, and from neorealist drama to social comedy—has paralleled the trajectory of Alea's directorial career. Similarly, Alea's films are a primary source of cultural politics in revolutionary Cuba, a fact that allows one to study his films directly against the political climate in which he lived and worked."

Dennis West added that "Tomas Gutiérrez Alea has been the most prominent of the filmmakers working in Cuba's government-supported film institute, the Instituto Cubano del Arte e Industria Cinematograficos (ICAIC). Gutiérrez Alea is a committed revolutionary, and his best features explore the social, political and historical dimensions of the revolutionary progress."

Solidarity served up with a cherry on top

After Cuba lost the socialist solidarity and trade it had had with the Soviet Union, the illegal U.S. blockade tightened its grip on the island's economy.

West pointed out in 1995, "Given the profound economic crisis currently gripping Cuba, it is astonishing that a feature such as 'Strawberry and Chocolate' could be produced. The situation in ICAIC is desperate. Top directors such as Gutiérrez Alea earn the approximate equivalent of $5.00 per month, and the once relatively well-funded ICAIC filmmakers can now undertake a feature only if co-production money is available. The low-budget 'Strawberry and Chocolate,' for instance, could not have been produced without Mexican and Spanish support."

Gutiérrez Alea, battling cancer, also had to undergo surgery during the production of the film. Juan Carlos Tabio, a collaborator, stepped up to co-direct the film.

"Strawberry and Chocolate" was the first Cuban movie to be nominated for an Oscar in the Best Foreign Film category. (Levin)

West concluded: "The commercial release of 'Strawberry and Chocolate' in the U.S. is a welcome event because U.S. authorities have at times hounded Gutiérrez Alea—by, for example, denying his visa requests or blocking exhibitions of his works. This interviewer's videotape copy of [Gutiérrez's 1968 film] 'Memories of Underdevelopment' was confiscated by U.S. Customs in Los Angeles when he entered the country on Dec. 11, 1993, after having legally attended the annual International Festival of New Latin American Cinema in Havana." By the closing ceremony of that festival in Havana on Dec. 10, 1993, "Strawberry and Chocolate" had won most of the top awards.

"Afterwards"—West, who was a guest, described—"in the Palace of the Revolution, Fidel Castro held a reception for festival guests featuring strawberry and chocolate ice cream served together for dessert." ▼

'Gay Cuba'

Two Cuban-backed documentaries about changing attitudes on the island towards same-sex love and gender variance—which in turn deepened that change—opened in theaters on the island in the mid-1990s.

"Gay Cuba" released in 1996 was a project of Cuba's Félix Varela Center (CFV). Activist Sonja de Vries—raised in Amsterdam and now living and organizing in Kentucky—wrote and directed the documentary, which objectively struck a blow against the political blockade of Cuba by U.S. imperialism.

"Gay Cuba" is a series of interviews—a radio host and a singer/poet, an artist and a gay male elected union general secretary, a feminine male factory worker and a journalist, an HIV-positive doctor and an interpreter, soldiers and teenaged law students—who offer personal anecdotes and individual observations about attitudes towards same-sex love in Cuba.

The interviews are interspersed with archival footage of the revolutionary seizure of power. The sound track incorporates the music of world-renowned Cuban musicians Pablo Milanés and Silvio Rodríguez.

The Cuban Women's Federation (FMC) hosted the opening screening of the documentary in Havana in 1994. The same year, the FMC invited an organization named "U.S. Queers for Cuba" to visit the island, the group's co-founder de Vries told Workers World.

"'Gay Cuba' was shown at the Havana International Festival of Latin American Cinema to public and critical acclaim," wrote scholar Larry R. Oberg.

The documentary turned its cameras onto the audiences of "Strawberry and Chocolate" (Fresa y chocolate), another film made with the help of the Cuban state. "Gay Cuba" captured some of the enthusiastic responses of Cubans who had just seen "Strawberry and Chocolate"—a 1993 film about a heterosexual communist and a homosexual Cuban—at the Yara cinema.

"Fantastic!" a filmgoer who described himself as a heterosexual, masculine male exclaimed. "If I could have a friend like that I would!"

Jorge Perugorria, a lead actor in "Strawberry and Chocolate," said in this documentary: "'Strawberry and Chocolate' is the story of an encounter ... between a communist militant and a homosexual, and how their friendship develops out of this encounter. What happened with the film is that it surpassed the cinematographic phenomena, and became a social phenomenon. People had never before discussed homosexuality so much."

Cuban journalist Gisela Arandia stressed in "Gay Cuba," "For people in other parts of the world, 'Strawberry and Chocolate' might be just another movie. For Cuba, it was an essential moment in our society's development, because never before had these topics been dealt with in public."

Measure of change

"Gay Cuba" was a weather vane that pointed in the direction of prevailing winds of change in the revolutionary battle against the legacy of centuries of colonialist and imperialist cultural domination.

These documentary interviews offered a cross-section of consciousness.

"They're people, one should treat them normally, but keep them away," one youth with her friends told the interviewer.

"They are part of our Cuban-ness, part of our people, we have to accept them as such," said an older man.

One young woman recalled going to a judgmental therapist about her attraction to other women. "I stood up, but first told him that he was mediocre and a bad psychologist and that I regretted being there. Then I stood up and left."

Another young woman remembered going to see a psychologist to try to change her same-sex attraction. "At the end of the week, she told me, 'Look, love, I see that you are happy as you are. Don't try to change. It's nothing out of this world. Nothing bad.'"

A cross-dressing factory worker explained, "Besides working here I am an artist. I imitate Sarita Montiel. I'm a drag queen. Everyone calls me 'Sarita.' My relationship with the workers here in the factory is wonderful. I've been here 12 years."

One young Cuban said when she was in high school, she thought that she was not accepted into the communist youth (UJC) group because there was discussion about whether she was or was not a lesbian.

Another Cuban emphasized, "I've read the statutes of the UJC, and I don't remember reading any article that said that being homosexual is an obstacle to being a member of the UJC. There are thousands of homosexuals in the UJC, from the roots to the leadership."

Lourdes Flores, from Cuba's National Center for Sex Education (CENESEX), stated in her interview, "As a center we see homosexuality as a sexual orientation, just like heterosexuality or bisexuality." She added, "We have led workshops on the topic of homosexuality; sexuality in general, homosexuality in particular. The workshops are very interesting. For example, we have workshops with teachers, doctors, the general population, community activists and youth."

"Gay Cuba" showed viewers a transgender performance organized by a neighborhood Committee for the Defense of the Revolution (CDR).

Cuban youth of all sexualities from Federation of University Students (FEU), Havana, March 1993. Still photo from the ground-breaking documentary 'Gay Cuba.'

'Break the blockade!'

The political views towards the revolution of those who spoke on camera in "Gay Cuba" largely could only be gleaned through their anecdotes. The individual experiences narrated in this documentary were positive and negative, in varying degrees.

Progress in Cuba is the measurable difference between the two.

It is painful to hear Llane Alexis Dominguez say onscreen that when his father found out he was homosexual, "He actually said he'd like to beat me to death!" In Cuba, however, men who have sex with men and women who have sex with women are not being tortured and lashed to fences to die, beaten to death, stabbed or shot or strangled, decapitated and dismembered—all too frequent occurrences in the U.S.

A gay male Cuban worker sums up that in Cuba in 1994 what was largely left to deal with were individual attitudes. "I don't think that Cuba's situation is as critical for gay people as it is in other countries," he explained. "I have the opportunity to study and to work here and no one can stop me. They might try to, but it's that individual, not the system itself."

He called on the gay community in the U.S. to help break the blockade, which, de Vries pointed out in her 1994 documentary commentary, "has cost the Cuban economy over $40 billion since 1960; the resulting fuel shortages and scarcity of food and medicine have impacted all Cubans."

Precious footage

The documentary also provides historic footage of Cuban *nova trova* singer Pablo Milanés singing his song "Original Sin" at a 1994 public concert in Havana. ("El Pecado Original" is available on Milanés's CD "Orígines.")

Milanés—a Cuban who harvested in the UMAP brigades in the mid-1960s, and who is beloved in Cuba—told the concert audience, "I dedicate this song to homosexuals, to gay people, and to all those who are marginalized and are suffering in the world."

Milanés sang: "Two souls, two bodies, two men who love each other, are being expelled from the paradise they live in. Neither of them is a warrior with victories to boast of. Neither of them has riches, to calm the ire of their judges. Neither is a president, neither is a censor of his own desires. We are not god. Let's not make the same mistakes again."

Larry Oberg noted, "Introduced at his annual holiday concert held in the vast Karl Marx Theater in the Miramar neighborhood of Havana, 'El Pecado Original' took the audience and the country by storm and did much to advance the cause of gay acceptance."

"Gay Cuba" includes footage documenting crossed-dressed homosexual Cubans participating in the annual, massive May Day march in 1995. Two lesbian and gay delegations were also invited from the U.S. to take part the same year. There's also footage of a lesbian and gay Cuban contingent in the José Martí procession.

At the close of "Gay Cuba," radio host Anna María Ramos concluded, "We have been in 35 years of revolution, a revolution that by no means has been static; that has made changes constantly. In every sense, we are prepared for change. The roots of homophobia have not been driven so deep into the soil of Cuban earth. They can be pulled out." ▼

Cross-gender performance in workers' dining halls

"Butterflies on the Scaffold" ("*Mariposas en el andamio*"), a 1995 documentary, offered a profoundly moving account of how Cuban women construction workers literally made room for cross-dressing performance art in the workers' cafeterias in their neighborhood on the outskirts of Havana, called La Güinera. The film was directed by Margaret Gilpin and Luis Felipe Bernaza.

Gilpin reported that the preliminary cut had to be shown 11 times at the Havana Film Festival in December 1995 to accommodate the crowds. In April 1996, the film won the best documentary and the popularity award at the lesbian and gay film festival in Turin.

The word "butterfly" ("mariposa") refers to male-bodied Cubans whose femininity is either a part or the whole of their gender expression. "Butterflies on the Scaffold" came out at the same time that a contingent of homosexual and gender-variant Cubans danced at the head of the massive May Day march in Havana that year. Two U.S. queer-focused activist delegations were invited to join in the procession—one from Bay Area Queers for Cuba, the other from New York's Center for Cuban Studies. (Hatch and DeVries)

Cuban women—"the revolution within the revolution"—made up 70 percent of the construction brigades that built La Güinera from the ground up.

For more than 15 years after the 1959 revolution, La Güinera remained undeveloped. The land was in the shadow of a meat factory, surrounded by bushes and insects.

Documentary footage explained that in the beginning, before government planning helped develop the community, "Squatters came from the provinces and formed an association. They said, we'll build your house today and mine tomorrow."

A local family doctor said to the interviewer, with pride, that by the time of this documentary, the local infant mortality rate in the neighborhood clinic. had dropped to two.

'We saw the show and we like it'

Marisela, a young woman of African descent on the construction staff, recalled that cross-dressing performance artists "had a show in a private house. They invited the girls from the [workers'] dining room. We went, we saw the group, the show, and we liked it."

One drag artist spoke from his home, the site of performances, explaining the early days of the shows. "We used sheets for fabric, no sequins, nothing. The dressing room was in the bedroom and we acted here. When the show moved to the backyard we used this as our dressing room. We had more room and air for us and for the public. The public brought their own chairs. Marisela even brought a sofa! In the short time we worked in my backyard this was the headquarters, the cradle of cross-dressing in Havana. Hundreds of drag queens came though here who never thought they would do this work."

The local security chief, on camera with his young daughter, expressed a backward view: "Personally, I don't think these things should increase. On the contrary, I think they should diminish. Children go there and see a person who is a man in normal life or who goes around as a man and later they see him dressed as a woman, that child will want to experiment and that's not what I want to see.

"Also, they charged admission for the parties they gave at home." A performer noted that the funds at one event were collected for the troops of the territorial militia—for the defense of Cuba.

The security police chief called off the drag shows. But that was not the end of the story.

Marisela explained, "After the police stopped the parties there was no place for them to perform. In solidarity I began to collect protest letters and petitions. The only option was Fifi. To bring them here so everyone could see them. I was convinced they were good."

Marisela was referring to the lead organizer of La Güinera's construction brigades—Josefina Bocourt Díaz, affectionately known as "Fifi."

'Fifi should be honored by us'

The woman whom co-workers and neighbors call "Fifi" is a Cuban of African descent. As a child, before the revolution, she had to start work at the age of 9. She explained, "I was one of the 70,000 maids that Cuba had before 1959. I couldn't enjoy much of my childhood. Now I've had the opportunity to work on the development of La Güinera and I feel like a new woman."

She narrated how her consciousness about transgender/homosexuality changed qualitatively while in a position of leadership.

Fifi remembered, "Marisela and the others came to see me. 'We want them in the cabaret. If you haven't seen them you can't object.'

"At first I rebelled," Fifi said, recalling her arguments: "I'm an older woman. I wasn't accustomed to running around with this 'class of people.' I said, 'No, keep them away. I don't want to hear about people who run around with a double façade.' ... I said, 'No, please, I can't be around you guys. I wouldn't be doing my duty to society. I'm too old for this stuff. I've never been involved in these things.'"

But Marisela persisted. She said, "Fifi, I saw a show. Fifi, they should start at once here in the workers' cafeteria."

The documentary 'Butterflies on the Scaffold' (Mariposas en el andamio) takes viewers to La Güinera, a neighborhood on the outskirts of Havana which has become a 'cradle of cross-dressing' in Cuba.

'Amigas.'

Margarita Gilpin

One drag performer said of Fifi, "She opened a cabaret in the workers' cafeteria and brought us into it. She made us face the 'herds' of public we were afraid to face. She reassured us. She said, "Do it, face them, you'll see, nothing will happen."

Another performer added, "Fifi should be honored by us. She'll always be close to our hearts for the wonderful way she treated us."

'A right to live as they wish'

This documentary was made during the "special period" in which Cuba had lost virtually all its trade when the USSR was overturned.

The U.S.-led economic blockade of Cuba also impacts on every aspect of life on the island: Performers use acetate because eyelash glue is not available. They create eyelashes out of horse hair or cut from carbon paper. Their nails are glued on with a shoe adhesive.

"Butterflies on the Scaffold" is packed with footage of indoor and outdoor drag performances in front of an audience of virtually all their co-workers and neighbors, family and friends. People of all ages attend the drag performances, arriving early for a good seat, or climbing onto a tree limb for a last-minute seat.

The performers take their bows to cheers and ovations.

A local congressional representative says, "[T]hey're giving the people something that others who aren't like them don't give."

A construction worker agreed. "They're the people who are giving this neighborhood a new level, a new character. Sometimes there's nothing to do and no place to go."

The performers play many other important roles in their community. They include a cook in a cafeteria for mechanics, a dentist, a baker, a dressmaker, a soldier just returned from an internationalist mission in Angola, a carpenter, a nurse, a horse trainer, a professor of Spanish literature and a professor of military topography.

These worker-sponsored drag shows in turn have been a fulcrum to lift consciousness about cross-dressing and male-bodied femininity and same-sex love. The process of change is apparent.

One young girl child of a cross-dressing performer, unequivocal and eloquent, told the interviewer: "I love my father with my life. I don't want anyone to be disrespectful to him. He's what he is. He wants to be that way, and he's a person and people have the right to live as they wish."

The child's parent, a drag performer, said, "I never deceived my kids. I tried to help them adapt to how things were, to how I felt—I never disguised myself as a 'man'—to know me as I am, to accept my friends. They need their own lives. My world is my world. But I don't want them to be estranged from who their father is and the work he does."

The pain in some families was palpable. One mother said when she found out her son was gay, "I felt real bad. Like all mothers, one wants the best for your children. We know he chose a difficult path … but in reality, it's not out of this world. … [H]e's my son and I would give my life for him."

A young man who says he is gay but not ready to do cross-dress performance said, "I have a fabulous family. They know all about me. They've known about me for 10 years and I'm 27. My family is exquisite. Up to now I haven't had problems. At first it was rough but once they realized it was my path, they accepted it and my friends, with their virtues and defects."

His father, working in the background, is asked, "What do you think of your son?"

The father answers, "No one's better. I couldn't ask for a better son. I'm grateful and proud he's my son. He's a good kid. He hasn't got any problems. He's A-1. Better than me and I'm his father."

After those words tumble out, the father and son hug each other.

The local doctor summed up, "The transvestite phenomenon marks a new era with perspectives for the union of humanity in love and mutual respect between human beings."

Fifi stressed, "I think this type of work should go on all over the country, because of the respect, pride and responsibility with which they work. If the nation accepts these cultural workers, these workers for the society, as we did here in La Güinera, we'll be successful as a nation."

Fifi concluded, "I think that our kids will grow up according to what we teach them. We have to explain the variety of life-styles in the world. They have to choose among them. If our kids get used to seeing men in drag, they'll see it as normal. We'll explain what a transvestite is and that child will choose a path to which their education leads and we'll create 'the new man.' Besides the new man will be brought up completely without any taboos!" ▼

1990s: Broadcasting education 'to every home'

The revolutionary Cuban government, since the 1990s, has waged a struggle against deep-rooted old prejudice about same-sex love in virtually every cultural venue.

In 1998 a national television program opened a mass discussion about lesbians and gays to immense audience interest. The topic was discussed in communities for weeks afterwards. (Hatch)

Oberg wrote on his observations of homosexuality and culture in Cuba: "Between March 2000 and April 2002, I spent more than four months in Cuba on four separate occasions, working as a librarian on a range of research projects with my Cuban colleagues. Most of that time was spent in Havana, but also in numerous other cities, including Matanzas, Trinidad and Santiago de Cuba. As a gay man, I was motivated to find out as much as I could about the status of Cuba's gay and lesbian population."

Oberg referred to the cross-dressing, cross-gender performances in the neighborhood of La Güinera, on the outskirts of the capital: "Many of these drag shows are sponsored by the local CDRs (Committees for the Defense of the Revolution)," Olberg reported, "and play to large and wildly enthusiastic audiences. (If you're wondering, the performers were great!)"

Oberg stressed, "One of the most striking things about Cuba is the vitality of its cultural and intellectual life throughout the island, particularly in Havana. Gay themes are prevalent in the theatre, in lectures, and in concerts.

"In December, 2000, I attended a play entitled 'Muerte en el Bosque' (A Death in the Woods), produced by the Teatro Sotano in Havana's Vedado neighborhood. Based upon the acclaimed novel 'Mascaras' (Masks), by Leonardo Padura Fuentes, the play follows a police investigation into the murder of a Havana drag queen, a plot device that allows for an examination of Cuban attitudes and prejudices towards gays at every level of society."

Oberg concluded, "A striking contradiction in Cuban society today is the contrast between the rich cultural and intellectual life that is widely available and easily affordable, and salaries that make the purchase of a pair of shoes an event for which one must plan."

He noted that Cubans could buy theater tickets for the equivalent of about a nickel, first-run movies for about a dime, theatrical plays for less than 50 cents, and musical extravaganzas and ballet festival performances for half a buck.

The U.S. blockade of Cuba, aimed at strangling the economy, makes it harder to buy a pair of shoes, let alone build socialism, which requires material abundance and often imported materials.

Wall Street hopes that economic deprivation will turn up the pressure cooker on internal relations, making it easier to wear down and overturn the revolution that took the Cuban economy, labor, land and resources off its list of neo-colonial "assets."

But the revolutionary government has continued to move forward on every front possible to generate consciousness, including about same-sex love.

"While in Cuba, I spoke with scores of gays, mostly men, and encountered none who said that their government was persecuting them," Oberg stated. He reiterated that no one with whom he spoke "reported active or systematic repression by the state."

Art and consciousness

AIDS prevention is only possible with widespread safer-sex information and a thoroughgoing struggle against sexual prejudices that allow the disease to spread in the silence of shame, guilt and fear. Revolutionary Cuban leadership brought the battle against AIDS and sexual prejudices—including bigoted attitudes about bisexuality—to the small screen of popular television, as well as the big screens of culture.

In 2006, the 115-chapter television series "The Hidden Face of the Moon" (La cara oculta de la luna), had virtually all of Cuba buzzing with debate. The series borrows from the popular style of television novellas—soap operas.

"La cara" deals with AIDS, youth sexuality, bisexuality and other social issues. The series began with the story of a 14-year-old girl who contracted AIDS during her first sexual experience.

As of November 2005, 5,422 Cubans were HIV-positive or had full-blown AIDS.

"La cara," wrote author Freddy Domínguez Díaz, was "a series on human behavior, on people's attitude of life, on everyone's responsibility for themselves and everybody else." (Betancourt)

Marlon Brito López, a screenwriter and director, critiqued the television novella "as a member of the audience and media expert." He wrote, "The main goals were well defined: a warning of the dangers of this pandemic disease, present also in our territory, which can infect people in any group, race or creed; and a reflection on the elimination of prejudice linked to HIV-AIDS and sex in our society, particularly within the family." (López)

Brito López stated, "I believe art is so ambiguous and abstract it has a latent effect on our consciousness, mainly when it reflects with honesty and talent the society one lives in. This is precisely what 'The Hidden Face of the Moon' is achieving."

He continued, "AIDS statistics in the world increased alarmingly and in our country; despite the excellent professional project and public health plan to prevent infectious diseases, media campaigns on the HIV-AIDS subject had shown little efficacy. It is here where we artists must step in. Concerts and songs by Buena Fe [Cuban musical group], or documentaries by my colleague Belkys Vega and others, were not enough to reach our homes at prime time with an artistically effective language, with affection and respect."

Bringing education to every home

"La cara" series director Rafael "Cheíto" González explained, "When we deal with present-day stories, we try to be as close to reality as possible. Everywhere in the world there are soaps for entertainment. We try to discuss the social problems we have and therefore we deal with topics such as these. I believe it is valid to face them with all seriousness. In this soap there are some parallel stories aimed only at entertaining the audience, but we cannot overlook the problems we have, and these must be tackled with courage.

"What better way to do it than through a TV soap watched by the whole country? Information on HIV is offered in TV spots, there is also a specific TV program on AIDS, but these are not seen by everybody. The soap, on the other hand, is watched in every home." (Puyol)

Cheíto noted, "We did a lot of research to pull out all the stops, as popular speech has it, in approaching AIDS as a topic, that is, seriously and with all due respect, since we can't beat about the bush if we want to send an effective message." (Betancourt)

Magda González, a television director who now directs the Dramatizations Division for Cuban TV, also stressed, "When we decided to take on this theme in this slot, we were convinced that it would provoke all sorts of reactions. They're not themes that we usually deal with in a dramatized form, even though over the past three years they have been dealt with in a direct and open way by other programs like 'Let's Talk about Health' (a weekly program talking about health matters) and 'It's Worthwhile' (a weekly program in which a leading psychologist discusses letter writers' problems)."

But as the AIDS epidemic continued, "and because we consider we have a socially responsible role to play to put television in the front line of the Battle of Ideas, we decided that the dramatic format was an ideal way to disseminate messages using the emotions and the viewer's identification with the human dramas. When writing the script and producing the tele-serial we called upon experts from the Center for Sexual Education (CENESEX) and the National HIV-AIDS Prevention Center as advisers and we believe it mirrors realistically aspects of our society.

"The second theme incorporates a new element in teledramas," she continued, "the treatment of sexual relations between men either as homosexuals or bisexuals. Public reaction is divided. Some are indignant that the theme is shown on screen, others applaud the initiative, and still others say that these themes have to be aired but not in this way.

"That the first exists is only natural in people whose sexual attitudes were formed by a Hispanic culture, heavily influenced by the Catholic Church, where sex is a sin and homosexuality a crime. Hopefully the telenovela will help them understand that to respect, recognize and tolerate different lifestyles doesn't turn them into accomplices of what they believe to be evil, but that it makes them followers of the concept given to us by our Co-mandante when he says that "The Revolution is about equality and full liberty, it's about being treated by everybody else as human beings." (Puyol)

This is revolutionary process

No one, of any sexuality, was of one mind in Cuba about "La cara." However, those who brought the series to television screens did not shy away from the debate. On the contrary, widespread public debate with leadership was the whole point, and it has been eminently successful.

The Cuban health-care system website "Infomed" garnered viewpoints about the television novella. So did Cuba's National Center for Sex Education (CENESEX). E-zine *La Jiribilla* devoted an entire issue to the topic.

Journalist Ricardo Ronquillo concluded, "It would be worrying if we thought of ourselves as a wholly agreeing society with neither competing arguments nor opposing positions in face of its most intimate conflicts; or even worse, that silence prevailed."

La Jornada correspondent Gerardo Arreola wrote, "This discussion has become the most relevant signs of public impact on the matter since the motion picture 'Fresa y Chocolate' ('Strawberry and Chocolate') shook sectors of Cuban society in 1993 with its statement against intolerance through the story of a homosexual character." (Arreola)

The *Miami Herald*, an unlikely source for any supportive news about Cuba, reported in November 2006, "Now, as the show draws to an end, Cuban gays and lesbians say the show is symbolic of the communist island's government and people becoming more accepting towards them." (See bibliography: "Cuban soap operas")

It is this process of popular education with leadership, in which consciousness is raised through mass participation, discussion and debate, that is the revolution and the "unfettered thought" it liberates—not overnight, but with ongoing labor, without which nothing is produced.

CENESEX continues to be at the forefront of that important work, including backing the television novella that sparked such controversy. ▼

Cuba's CENESEX leads the way on sexual rights

Cuba's National Center for Sex Education (Centro Nacional de Educación Sexual) carries out its important collective labor—including combating what remains of pre-revolutionary prejudice against same-sex love—in what was once a privately owned Havana mansion.

Mariela Castro Espín, director of CENESEX, stressed that sexologists have a "scientific, social and political responsibility" to help raise understanding and consciousness in the whole population. (havanajournal.com, April 1, 2003)

CENESEX's goal, Castro Espín explained, is to contribute to "the development of a culture of sexuality that is full, pleasurable and responsible, as well as to promote the full exercise of sexual rights." (Reed)

Since she and CENESEX are part of the revolution, they don't have to do this work alone.

"Historically speaking," Castro Espín stated, "changing mentality is one of the most difficult things to do, one of the slowest processes in society. Even though we've made substantial political and legislative strides, we're still bound by aspects of roles defined long ago. This subjectivity begins early, in the way children are raised, in how they're taught to play.

"We have to learn to recognize which elements of the traditional masculinity or femininity are actually doing us damage. What parts of the picture actually take away from our freedom, fulfillment and dignity. We have to take a hard look at these things, or else we'll keep passing them down from generation to generation." (Reed)

She offered a concrete example about AIDS safer-sex education. "We have to include a gender perspective—promotion of new constructs of masculinity and femininity—and not just take an epidemiological approach."

She said an epidemiological approach to prevent AIDS transmission might simply suggest, "Use a condom."

But the system of male chauvinism imposed on Cuba for centuries created a mindset in which some males feel that condoms may be a sensation barrier to full sexual enjoyment, to which they are entitled. Castro Espín emphasized, "So, for him to use a condom, he has to begin to construct and define his masculinity in a different way, that doesn't put a premium only on his own pleasure. In the end, this stereotype is very dangerous to his own health as well as his partner's—and this can be true for homosexual as well as heterosexual couples, whenever a relationship defines that one partner has hegemony over the other.

"So you need to combine both an epidemiological and a gender approach to these very intimate issues. This is why, for example, our posters and other materials emphasize that protection of your partner against HIV and STIs in general is a sign of caring, and that means it's a responsibility of both partners in a relationship."

Castro Espín told *MEDICC Review* interviewer Gail A. Reed regarding CENESEX, "We work with groups who promote safe sex among their peers: men who have sex with men [MSM], transvestites and transsexuals, adolescents and young people in general and then more broadly with medical students. In each medical school, there's a department of Sexology and Education for Sexuality."

All education in Cuba, it bears repeating—including medical school—is free.

Castro Espín observed in 2006, "Regarding attitudes towards MSM and bisexuals as well, there have been positive changes—I say empirically, since we are still studying this. But at our conferences and workshops that we hold with people from the whole country, it's clear that participants are more able now than 10 years ago to understand and respect another sexual orientation. I think the work that's been done over the decade in health and by the Cuban Women's Federation has helped to bring about that change, and we've done it reaching out to people's sensitivity as human beings.

"In essence, our view is that any kind of prejudice or discrimination is damaging to health." (Reed)

'Modifying the social imagination'

As a revolutionary worker, Castro Espín demonstrates in every interview that she has already rolled up her sleeves to do the next job that needs to be done.

She talked about the revolutionary labor that is still required to make progress in overcoming old prejudices about same-sex love. "First," she told Reed, "I think we have to work more and better in the schools. We've worked with the Ministry of Education, but I'm still not satisfied we've made enough progress, and so we need to deepen understanding among teachers and other school staff; we need to carry more on educational TV and so on.

"And this also has to do with a gender focus, of course. In the 70s and 80s, we found a lot of fear and resistance to a national program for sex education with such a gender focus. The program was finally accepted in 1996, and now it's taught throughout the country; since then it has reduced school dropouts from early marriages and childbirth by one half."

Castro Espín elaborated, "The country now has policies that legitimize sexual orientations and also has brought laws in line with a gender perspective. But on the legislative front, there is still a lot to be done."

She has proposed that when the Cuban Constitution of the Republic is next revised, the category of "sexual orientation" be added. Castro Espín said homosexual Cubans are protected, but "when something like that is made explicit, it is official recognition that there is a need to avoid any type of discrimination, like racism or sexism."

Such a legal measure, she pressed, would make this protection even more evident. And, she added, it's important to protect against discrimination, not just in public institutions "but also in the space of the family, because it is often there that a homosexual is first insulted or rejected."

No Cuban of any sex has to marry in order to have economic support, a job, a home, health care or other rights that are guaranteed to every person. Castro Espín pointed out, though, that although homosexuals live within the law in consensual relationships, "gay marriage is not recognized, so you have many issues such as inheritance that aren't fully resolved. We need changes in the family code itself related to these and other questions, including domestic violence. CENESEX has now presented two bills in Parliament before the education and children's commissions that have to do with gender," she noted, "and these have been well received."

Unofficial same-sex marriages have taken place on the island. For example, four local young males ranging in ages from 17 to 22 held a double same-sex ceremony outdoors, in front of loved ones and neighbors, in the working-class suburb of San Miguel del Padrón, southeast of Havana, in 2001. (Berkowitz, Cabral)

Castro Espín summed up, "By the 1970s, reforms to the penal code excluded the classification of homosexuals as criminals (because of their sexual orientation); any word that discriminated against homosexuals was modified.

"However," she stressed, "that is not enough because I think our laws should better reflect the respect that homosexuals deserve. Greater and more professional work is needed at the micro-social level, because what this is about is trying to change perceptions, modifying the social imagination." (Garcia) ▼

Teresa Gutierrez

Leslie Feinberg, shortly after initiating the Rainbow Solidarity for the Cuban Five Campaign, presents Cuban Ambassador Rodrigo Malmierca Díaz with copies of her books.

Cuba's CENESEX proposes ground-breaking transsexual rights

Mariela Castro Espín, director of Cuba's National Center for Sex Education (CENESEX), recalled that three decades ago a Cuban from Matanzas who was born female-bodied but identified as male came to Havana for help.

In response, Cuban revolutionary leader and president of the Federation of Cuban Women (FMC), Vilma Espín, recommended in 1979 that a special committee be established, coordinated by the National Work Group on Sex Education—CENESEX's predecessor. The FMC had formed the Work Group in 1972; CENESEX was established in 1989.

The first result, Castro Espín related, was an agreement with the Ministry of the Interior and the Ministry of Justice to issue new identity papers. Three transsexual Cubans got new identity documents under that accord.

In 1988, the first sex-reassignment surgery—from male to female—was carried out successfully in Cuba. The operation was successful and the person reportedly lives without difficulty.

But the media coverage, Castro Espín remembered, was tinged with more sensationalism than science. Historically unchallenged prejudice welled up. As a result, the CENESEX director explained, the operations were temporarily halted until the need for them could be explained to the population. Clinical and psychological care continued for transsexual Cubans, but with a lower profile.

Castro Espín stated in the January 2006 *La Jornada* interview, "We were unable to convince people of the need to carry out these operations. This reluctance also came from the professionals in the Ministry of Public Health who were not experts on the subject. This is where I feel the strongest resistance, even as we speak."

Journalist Gerardo Arreola added that in recent years, "A group of transsexuals joined CENESEX and were trained as sex health promoters in the campaign for the prevention of AIDS. In the center they have a permanent open debate forum and receive specialized care. The health system provides them with free hormone treatment."

Sex change and social change

"At the beginning of 2004," Arreola wrote, "there was a new momentum when CENESEX launched a national strategy: it increased and diversified its professional staff, obtained support from President Fidel Castro and directly contacted ministries and social organizations to discuss, based on entity profile, the subject of transsexuals."

Two years later, Castro Espín said, this move has accelerated change. "It seems all this work is now bearing fruit. People are now more receptive. We have also articulated a more persuasive discourse. I see great flexibility, even among official leaders."

Castro Espín, as director of CENESEX, took a plan about expanding rights for transsexuals to two parliamentary committees on Dec. 20, 2005.

Granma reported the following day that CENESEX had "released results of a survey on gender identity in today's Cuban society to the committees on Education, Culture, Science, Technology and the Environment, and Youth, Children and Women's Rights.

"Mariela Castro said that for people with a non-traditional gender identity to fully develop their potential as a member of society, it is first necessary to identify them so as to assure that they receive adequate specialized assistance. She also noted the need in Cuban society of a profound understanding of gender and sexuality."

Correspondent Gerardo Arreola interviewed Castro Espín, in the Jan. 9, 2006, issue of *La Jornada*, about the move to widen rights for transsexuals. Castro Espín outlined that her proposal to parliament would make free sex reassignment surgery and hormones available to all transsexual Cubans—all forms of health care are provided cost-free on the island. New identity documents would also be immediately issued.

Arreola reported, "This is part of a national policy to recognize the rights of these people to live a full life in the gender they chose."

Castro Espín stated, "The draft was very well received by the representatives in the two commissions examining the project." She added, "They not only accepted the proposal, but asked many questions and made recommendations."

By 2006, a transsexual Cuban woman traveled abroad on her new passport. Four others who had sex reassignment surgeries abroad got changed identity papers as soon as they returned home. "The Courts of Justice were finally convinced," Castro Espín concluded.

In early 2007, Cuba's National Assembly of Popular Power agreed to discuss making sex-reassignment surgery free of cost to all transsexuals on the island who request it.

The newsletter "Diversity" (Diversidad) reported: "The measure would complement the present Identity Law that already acknowledges the right of citizens to change name and sexual identity. This places Cuba at the vanguard of the legislations that acknowledge the rights of transvestites, transsexuals and transgender in Latin America." ("Cuban Parliament")

In fact, by also providing free health care, Cuba is truly leading the world in rights for transsexual and gender-variant people.

Revolution takes work

Mariel Castro Espín and CENESEX don't rest on these laurels. She emphasized the need for legislation and other actions to block discrimination and raise popular consciousness.

A job is a right in Cuba. However, she said, "there may be transsexuals who have a job and are not rejected, because the law protects them, even if they go cross-dressed. But the administrators always find a way to get rid of them."

Addressing a conflict between revolutionary security police and trans Cubans two years earlier, Castro Espín was very clear. She stated that neighbors had complained about street solicitation. But when the security police arrested transsexuals and transvestites, based on an assumption that they were prostitutes, Castro Espín stressed that they were acting on backward ideas and prejudice.

"The police take measures—that's what they are there for," she explained, "but they interpret things with their own way of thinking. They have learned over their lifetimes that transsexuals and homosexuals are intrinsically bad." (Rodriquez)

"This attitude was not in keeping with the policy or the law, because these do not penalize a person for cross-dressing." (Arreola)

Castro Espín noted, "We have been given procedural guidelines so these people know how to defend themselves in case of police transgression of the regulations." (Arreola)

She explained that CENESEX intervened and set up a channel of communication with the revolutionary security forces and the Ministry of the Interior. Together they ordered police not to hassle transgender and transsexual Cubans. They also agreed to provide education to Cuba's National Revolutionary Police, including a seminar on distinct expressions of gender and sexuality. (Arreola)

Castro Espín noted that the transsexual and transgender Cubans who had been harassed came right to CENESEX to lodge complaints and demand redress. "Of course, they came to demand their rights, because I don't know if you have noticed, we Cubans have a strong sense of justice and fight when we have to," she said. (González)

"They spoke of everything that bothered them. I asked if I could tape what they had said to prepare a report. And that's what I did; a short report so they could read it over rapidly and then a longer one with many annexes.

"That is how a national strategy came about for attention to transsexuals with an integral vision since 1979, which was created by my mother, Vilma Espín, president of the Cuban Women's Federation. What we did was to broaden this work, to enrich it." (Mariela Castro Espín's father is acting Cuban President Raul Castro.)

"We are even carrying out a very important study on representations of transsexuality," she concluded, "to carry out educational campaigns to teach society to respect these people and respect their rights." (González) ▼

Ricardo Alarcon, president of Cuba's National Assembly, stated in spring 2007: 'We have to abolish any form of discrimination' against homosexuality. He explained, 'We are trying to see how to do that, whether it should be to grant them the right to marry or to have same-sex unions. We have to redefine the concept of marriage. Socialism should be a society that does not exclude anybody.'

Cuba: 'Bringing revolution's humanity to all aspects of life'

"I want to bring the revolution's humanity to those aspects of life that it hasn't reached because of old prejudices," Mariela Castro Espín, who has worked hard to eradicate pre-revolutionary prejudices about same-sex love, transsexuality and gender variance in Cuba, said in summer 2006. (Israel)

Castro Espín is director of Cuba's National Center for Sex Education (CENESEX), which has accomplished a great deal in a relatively short time to replace prejudices about same-sex love and transsexuality with positive attitudes.

CENESEX created its own Internet web site—www.cenesex.sld.cu—shortly after the 16th World Congress of Sexology met in Havana in March 2003.

CENESEX's site incorporates a section on sexual diversity, which offers in Spanish and English basic information, opportunities to consult with experts, and voicing of public opinion.

The site gets right to the point about its objective, which it states is to "overcome the taboos and prejudices that persist about same-sex love: Being homosexual or bisexual is not a disease, it is not synonymous with perversity, nor does it constitute a crime."

Homosexuality, the web site makes clear, "is a sexual orientation that is not caused by seduction at any age, it is not contagious, and is not acquired by educational defects or negative examples in the family environment."

This Internet site receives the most visits—150,000 "hits" a day—of any Cuban World Wide Web portal. (IPS/GIN, July 3, 2004)

Castro Espín said in the summer of 2004 that these developments are "the result of an effort of more than 30 years, and now we are seeing its fruits more clearly." (Acosta)

Work accomplished, work to do

When asked by a BBC reporter in September 2006 whether perceptions about homosexuality had changed in Cuban society, Mariela Castro Espín answered, "I think so; it has changed very much." (González)

She told interviewer Eduardo García Jiménez, "I do believe that since the 1990s there is greater acceptance of the presence of homosexuals by some portion of the population and public institutions. That does not mean that the contradiction has been resolved for all individuals at all levels of society.

Castro Espín added, "I think we are at a good moment to implement policies that are more explicit about the defense of the human rights of homosexuals, so that we are better prepared to confront any manifestation of discrimination on the grounds of sexual orientation. I see this very humanistic attempt to achieve greater respect for the rights of homosexuals as the waging of a battle of ideas in our society. I believe this notion has to be part of the cultural and political battle because that would mean a cultural, social and political strengthening for the Cuban Revolution."

Castro Espín said she is advocating for an amendment to the Cuban Constitution to add homosexuality to the groups against which discrimination is outlawed. "It is a proposal I am making from my position of responsibility as the director of the CENESEX. I assure you it has been heard by receptive listeners. My proposal is in no way removed or distant from the spirit of the revolution, or from the entire process that has brought about this call to a battle of ideas.

"It would be wonderful to be able to spark meaningful, inter-group discussion on this subject," Castro Espín emphasized, "so that Cuban society could develop a healthier culture of sexuality, one that is fairer, that helps to erode old, erroneous beliefs and prejudices that emphasize sexual orientation.

"Something like this would put the revolution even more in line with its humanistic ethic; the Cuban Revolution has been possible because of the participation of all men and women, of all Cubans who have identified with the conquests and dreams of that social project. Among all those who have participated there are also people of diverse sexual orientations."

Don't measure with imperial ruler

As earlier articles in this series documented, the CIA, Hollywood and corporate media tried to deflect resistance to U.S. imperialism's covert war against Cuba, and its domestic discrimination, police brutality and bashing of same-sex-loving and gender-variant people, by focusing on the onerous tasks Cuba's revolution faced in uprooting centuries of prejudice about same-sex love. Of course, each poisonous seed had been planted and cultivated by U.S. capitalism and, earlier, Spanish colonialism.

However, Castro Espín stated categorically to journalist Mary Lamey via a translator, "There is no official repression of lesbians and gays in Cuba. What remains are social and cultural reactions that must be transformed, the same as in many other countries." (Lamey)

She pointed to the bashings of transsexuals and homosexuals in England and other imperialist countries: "This doesn't exist in Cuba. The Cuban population is much more respectful of differences than in other places." She emphasized, "When I'm afraid I will find a very strong resistance, I find a high degree of sensibility in the Cuban population."

Today, the Cuban Revolution has made enormous strides in raising popular consciousness about sexual liberation, including same-sex love. Building ties of unity will require conscious leadership of the most resolutely anti-imperialist activists in the liberation movement for LGBT and other sexually, sex- and gender-oppressed peoples.

Yet some activists in the U.S. still argue that Cuba won't have "passed the test" until lesbians and gays are "out" in Cuba with their own autonomous organizational formations.

Cubans defining their own liberation

In a capitalist country, being "out" is not only an assertion of individual identity and personhood. The movement to end the oppression has to be "out" and independent, as well. That is because of the LGBT movement's relationship to its own ruling class in capitalist countries. In the class struggle, it is imperative for the movement to break free of its own capitalist bosses and their ideology. In that case, the movement is only as powerful as it is independent.

But what about a socialist country in which the laboring class rules and is trying to build socialism in the liberated turf of a workers' state?

An international network of both LGBT social democrats and those far to the right of them in the imperialist countries, particularly the U.S. and Britain, makes an appeal to Cubans, and others in countries menaced by imperial powers, to identify with them based on what is presumed to be shared identity. In turn, this network asserts its readiness to defend gay and lesbian Cubans and others—but only against their own people, culture and national liberation struggle.

When aligned with overall and sometimes specific imperialist interests, such a position can offer a "left cover" for regime change—through covert and/or military intervention.

Defend Cuba!

Cubans are defining their own liberation.

The Cuban Revolution merits the support of progressives and communists around the world, without demands that it measure up as "perfect" using an imperial ruler. A socialist revolution is a process, not a single act. Solving the economic and social problems that the capitalists cannot and will not tackle is the dynamic forward motion of revolution.

Regarding the revolution's efforts to eliminate old prejudice against homosexuality, Fidel Castro concluded during a 1988 interview with a Galician television station: "Given that we can make mistakes, we obsessively follow the idea [of] what is just, right and best for the people, and what is most humane for our people and our society. However, the task is not easy—I think that each time we get closer to the right criteria for making the world we want. Nonetheless, I think that we still have many faults, and that future generations will have to continue to perfect this new world." (Hillson)

The whole population of Cuba—of all races, sexes, genders, sexualities, ages and abilities—does not need to be defended against its own culture or its own revolution. It needs and deserves defense against the U.S. blockade of its island and every other illegal act of imperialist war, overt and covert, which impedes revolutionary progress.

International support for Cuba's right to sovereignty and self-determination will allow the island's population to spend more time, energy and resources on socialist construction, rather than on defense.

It is the LGBT movements in the imperialist citadels that have to break with their own ruling classes in order to build bonds of genuine international solidarity. It's a hard position to take. It requires ideological valor; the refusal to remain silent about the emperor's "new" clothing.

The Cuban Revolution has had to take up the tasks that history presented it, including the eventual eradication of the legacies of racism, sexism and anti-gay bigotry.

In order to move forward toward their own liberation, the LGBT and other progressive movements in the U.S. and other capitalist countries have to combat anti-communism—which is, in the long run, a loyalty oath to capitalism—and develop a powerful anti-imperialist current that can extend its solidarity to Cuba and all countries fighting for their sovereignty and self-determination against finance capital.

Revolutionary Cuba—the "hope of the hemisphere"—has done a better job dealing with its tasks. ▼

Rainbow Solidarity for Cuban Five circles globe

A multi-national, multi-lingual group of lesbian, gay, bisexual and trans (LGBT) activists in the United States—the belly of the beast—issued a call in Spanish and English for Rainbow Solidarity for the Cuban Five in mid-January 2007.

The five political prisoners—Gerardo Hernández, Antonio Guerrero, Ramón Labañino, Fernando González and René González—are collectively serving four life sentences and 75 years in far-flung U.S. penitentiaries. The "crime" they were convicted of is having infiltrated CIA-backed fascist commando groups in order to halt terror attacks against Cuba from U.S. soil.

The Rainbow Solidarity call demands a new trial and freedom for these political prisoners, defense of Cuban sovereignty and self-determination and a halt to the illegal U.S. acts of war against Cuba—including the economic blockade and CIA trained, funded and armed attacks by mercenary "contra" armies operating from this country.

This initiative was consciously issued by LGBT and other activists battling oppression based on sexuality, gender expression and sex—one of the progressive movements targeted by the imperialist campaign to vilify Cuba.

This was not the first act of solidarity with Cuba by left-wing LGBT activists in the United States—not by a long shot. But the response to the Rainbow Solidarity initiative—swift and dramatic—signals a new day for LGBT support worldwide for Cuba.

Within hours and days after the call went out over the Internet, hundreds of individuals and organizations signed on to the call, posted on the www.nyfreethefive.org web site (look for the rainbow).

Most exciting was how many of the signers immediately began forwarding the call to their e-mail lists.

Volunteers from around the world translated the introduction and call for Rainbow Solidarity to free the Cuban Five into simplified and traditional Chinese, Tagalog, Farsi, Turkish, Greek, Croatian, Portuguese, Italian, Danish, Japanese, French and German. More translations in the works or planned include Swahili, Urdu, Indonesian, Arabic, Korean, Bengali and a streaming video in ASL (American Sign Language).

International endorsements flooded in from Argentina, Australia, Austria, Belgium, Brazil, Canada, Costa Rica, Croatia, Cuba, Cyprus, Denmark, England, Finland, France, Germany, Greece, India, Iran, Ireland, Italy, Japan, Luxemburg, Mexico, Montenegro,

New Zealand, occupied Palestine, Philippines, Portugal, Puerto Rico, Romania, Scotland, Serbia, Spain, Sweden, Switzerland, Turkey, United Arab Emirates, Wales and other countries and nations and from Hong Kong and Taiwan.

Individuals and groups from every state in the continental U.S. signed on as well—from southern Florida to the Pacific Northwest, Southern California to Maine.

All told, they form an extraordinary and broad arc of a united front. A frequently updated list of signers is posted at www.freethefiveny.org.

Many names on the growing list will be recognizable as well-known LGBT activists and others battling oppression based on sexuality, gender and sex, including women's liberationists.

This roster also reveals that many of these activists are also some of the hardest-working organizers in movements here and around the world against imperialist war, neo-liberalism, neo-colonialism, national oppression, racism, police brutality, prison and death penalty abolition, sweatshops and capitalist globalization.

These are also leading activists in the struggle for immigrant rights; women's liberation, including reproductive rights; jobs; labor union, tenant and community organizing; education; health care and affordable housing; freedom for all U.S. political prisoners and for prisoner rights; liberation of oppressed nations; support for Cuba, and the revolutionary movement to overturn capitalism and build an economy based on planning to meet peoples' needs.

Expansive political spectrum

Early signers include Teresa Gutierrez, a long-time leader in the struggle to free the Cuban Five; former political prisoner and leading prison abolitionist Angela Y. Davis; Leslie Cagan, national coordinator of United for Peace and Justice; LeiLani Dowell, national coordinator of FIST (Fight Imperialism, Stand Together); Stephen Funk, the U.S. Marine who was the first imprisoned Iraq War conscientious objector; Bev Tang, organizer for Anakbayan, the youth group of Bayan; Gerry Scoppettuolo, co-founder of GALLAN (Pride At Work, Boston); Lani Ka'ahumanu, BiNET USA; anti-imperialist activist Joo-Hyun Kang; Atlanta community activist Pat Hussain; Camille Hopkins, director of NYTRO (New York Transgender Rights Organization) of Western New York; transgender activist Moonhawk River Stone; and Jesse Lokahi Heiwa, Queer People Of Color Action.

Rauda Morcos, general coordinator of Aswat-Palestinian Gay Women, signed on. The Puerto Rican Alliance of Los Angeles and its coordinator Lawrence Reyes have endorsed.

Activists Barbara Smith and Margo Okazawa-Rey signed. The two were among the founders of the Combahee River Collective, a group of Black feminists of all sexualities who issued a historic 1977 statement against the "interlocking" system of "racial, sexual, heterosexual and class oppression."

Former political prisoners Laura Whitehorn and Linda Evans added their names.

Louisville, Ky., filmmaker and activist Sonja de Vries, director of the documentary "Gay Cuba," and Walter Lippmann, editor-in-chief of CubaNews, signed on. Other activists and organizations working in defense of Cuba also added weight to the call, including Cuba Education Tours, Vancouver, B.C., Canada; Fairness Campaign, Louisville, Ky.; Simon McGuinness, secretary of the Free the Miami Five Campaign, Ireland; Brigitte Oftner, coordinator of the Austrian Free the Five committee; Viktor Dedaj, webmaster of the Cuba Solidarity Project; the Cuba Edmonton Solidarity Committee in Alberta, Canada; the Swiss Cuba Association; Deutsche Kommunistische Partei Cuba Arbeits-gruppe, Germany; and No War on Cuba, Washington, D.C.

Groups include the national organization Pro-Gay Philippines; Audre Lorde Proj-ect—a Lesbian, Gay, Bisexual, Two Spirit and Transgender People of Color center for community organizing, focusing on the New York City area; FIERCE!—a community organization for Transgender, Lesbian, Gay, Bisexual, Two Spirit, Queer, and Question-ing (TLGBTSQQ) youth of color in New York City; QUIT! (Queers Undermining Israeli Terrorism); LAGAI-Queer Insurrection; Stonewall Warriors, Boston; Greek Homosexual Community, Athens, Greece; Queertoday.com, Boston, Mass.; and Queers Without Borders, Hartford, Conn.

The Queer Caucus of the National Lawyers Guild; Stephen Whittle, professor of equalities law and the British organization Press for Change at the School of Law at Manchester Metropolitan University, endorsed. So did Barbara Findlay, co-chair of the Lesbian Gay Bisexual and Transgender Issues Section, BC Branch, Canadian Bar As-sociation; and the law office of Lenore Rae Shefman, San Francisco, Calif.

Many transgender and transsexual organizations and individuals strengthened the initiative, including Trans Action Canada; three national Italian trans groups: Coordina-mento Nazionale Trans FTM, Movimento Identità Transessuale and Crisalide Azione Trans; playwrite and performer Imani Henry; Matt/ilda a.k.a. Matt Bernstein Syca-more, editor "Nobody Passes," San Francisco, Calif.; Cianán Russell, chair of the Indiana Transgender Rights Advocacy Alliance; and the Winona Gender Mutiny Collective.

Endorsers include The National Lavender Green Caucus; Doug Barnes and the Freedom Socialist Party; Starlene Rankin, Green National Committee delegate of the Lavender Caucus of the Green Party of the United States; Orange County Peace & Freedom Party, Anaheim, Calif; and the LGBT Caucus of Workers World Party.

Among the signers are individuals and organizations whose activist work includes the struggle against women's oppression: Brenda Stokely, a leader of the Million Worker March Movement and NYCLAW; transnational feminist theorist Chandra Talpade Mo-hanty; Sara Flounders, co-director of the International Action Center; Women's Fight-back Network, Boston, Mass.; Melinda Clark, local co-founder of Code Pink in Willits, Calif.; Welfare Warriors, Milwaukee, Wis.; League of Women Voters in Montenegro; and

Women's International League for Peace and Freedom (WILPF) chapters in Washington, D.C.; Rome, Italy; and the Canadian Section in British Columbia.

Many LGBT labor activists have added their names and/or the endorsement of their unions, including the Pride at Work/GALLAN (Gay and Lesbian Labor Action Network), Boston, Mass, AFL-CIO; Bus Riders Union/Labor Community Strategy Center, Los Angeles, Calif.; and from Canada: Canadian Union Of Postal Workers, Calgary, Alberta; Canadian Union of Public Employees, Toronto, Ont.; and Hospital Employees' Union, Burnaby, B.C.

There's no end in sight to this rainbow.

Grassroots diplomacy

The Rainbow Solidarity for the Cuban Five initiative is also giving voice to individuals who, living in capitalist democracies, have little political input.

The Rainbow Solidarity call has become a poll that reveals a new grassroots sentiment as signers eloquently register their outrage at the continued imprisonment of the five Cubans and at Washington's economic and political blockade of Cuba and other illegal and covert acts of war.

Rebecca writes from San Diego, Calif., "Free the Cuban Five!! No more political prisoners!"

David from New York State stresses how biased the trial venue was for the Five: "[The] Five Cubans were trying to stop the ultra-right terrorist groups in Miami from carrying out violent actions against the people of Cuba. Miami is the one city in the U.S. where the Five certainly could not receive a fair trial."

Paul says: "As a gay man in South Florida who calls for freedom for our brothers, the Five, I am delighted to see this initiative. THEY MUST BE FREE!"

Tighe supports the five as "those most important defenders of everyone's right to live without fear of terrorism. The patriotic Cuban Five [are] illegally held political prisoners in a country with the most of its own people behind bars."

Barry, who grew up in Miami, adds the need to organize to close down the U.S. prison at Guantanamo and free all those held there.

"T." from California comments, "These five men, fighting against terrorism, have been imprisoned by the U.S. government—'MY' government! Jailing heroes and supporting terror, while pretending to do the opposite, is sadly all the public can count on from 'our' hypocritical, double-speaking, global corporate-run excuse for a 'by and for the people' government."

Brian states from Newport, Ore., "I am enraged by the hypocrisy of five innocent men being held in prison under harsh circumstances while known terrorist Luis Posada Carriles goes scot-free. While Bush and cronies spout off that no nation that harbors terrorists will be tolerated with one face, they set a convicted terrorist murderer of at least 73 innocents free with the other, while holding five innocent men in prison."

Adela, from the Zig Zag Young Women's Resource Centre Inc. in Queensland,

Australia, states, "I want to express my solidarity with the Cuban Five and the Cuban people and Fidel."

Richard, from Madera, Calif., says succinctly, "It's way past time to change our policy toward Cuba and the Cuban people."

Jerry, from Athletes United for Peace, U.S.-El Salvador Sister Cities, Nicaragua Solidarity Committee, writes: "These people were trying to prevent an act of terrorism. The country that claims to lead the 'War On Terror' is imprisoning them."

Marcos writes from Bielefeld, Germany, "Free the Five Cubans now, stop the war on Cuba and the rest of the world!"

Richard, in Jacksonville, Ill., says, "Close Guantánamo, human rights are for humans everywhere."

Ray from Farmington, Conn., suggests, "Put Cheney and Bush in jail instead of the Cuban Five."

Yancy, from the LGBTQI Desk of Bayan USA, affirms: "Mabuhi ang panaghiusang international!!! Long live international solidarity!!"

Solidarity is not charity

Eric from Milwaukee reminds, "Ah, the things we gain from solidarity."

It is in the interests of LGBT activists and organizations in the U.S. and other imperialist countries to break with their own ruling classes and extend their own unilateral declaration of peace to a socialist country. And by rejecting anti-communism, the movement against sexual, gender and sex oppression can combat capitalist ideology—a giant step towards liberation.

Cuba has much to teach those who yearn for the right to live and love without fear or censure about what it takes to begin the process of literally eradicating white supremacy, patriarchy and prejudice against same-sex love and gender/sex diversity; what it takes to create a new woman, a new man, a new human being, and new forms of communist comradeship.

The Cuban people fought back against enslavement for half a millennium. For the last half century they have resisted the most powerful slave-master in history, just 90 miles from their shores.

The famous labor union song poses the question sharply: Which side are you on?

Rainbow Solidarity answers: "*Cuba, estamos contigo*. Cuba we are with you." ▼

Alicia González of the Federation of Cuban Women (Federación de Mujeres Cubanas, FMC) holds up gift of first Rainbow Solidarity for the Cuban Five poster presented by Leslie Feinberg at a Workers World Party International Women's Day commemoration meeting March 9, 2007 in New York City.

Tami Starlight, director of Trans Action Canada: *"I support this fully!"*

Lynda, from Elk, Calif.: *"Please add my name to the call to free the Cuban 5 (I am a lesbian)."*

Tim: *"My partner and I are with you 100 percent."*

Joan, from Brooklyn, N.Y.: *"I have long been outraged by the terrible injustice of their situation."*

Larry of the Scottish Socialist Freedom Movement: *"It is time these Cubans had a fair trial and it is recognized they were protecting their homeland from U.S.-sponsored terrorism."*

Richard from Wappingers Falls, N.Y., states, *"It is wrong, it is immoral and unjust what the U.S. is doing to these five men."*

Jay, from Shrewsbury, England, emphasizes, *"It's about time they were out of there and back home."*

Sandy, from Paterson, N.J., says, *"This is a miscarriage of justice."*

G. Dunkel

First public event for Rainbow Solidarity for the Cuban Five at the New York City LGBT Community Center on June 2, 2007. From left: Helena Wong, Benjamin Ramos, Leslie Feinberg, LeiLani Dowell, Joan Gibbs, Teresa Gutierrez and Yancy Mark Gandionco (not seen in this photo) applauded Secretary Jorge Luis Dustet from the United Nations Cuban Mission as he holds up poster with the names of the first 1,000 signers of the call for Rainbow Solidarity with the Cuban Five.

You can make the call for Rainbow Solidarity for the Cuban Five more powerful by adding your name at: www.nyfreethefive.org. Please help circulate the call far and wide, on the Internet, at your campus, community organization, local Pride events and other activities.

Translations, downloadable leaflets, posters and buttons are available online.

Rainbow Solidarity organizers stress that to make this call even more powerful, your signature is needed. To become a part of Rainbow Solidarity to Free the Cuban Five, sign on at: www.nyfreethefive.org/rainboweng.htm.

For ideas about how to deepen this initiative, e-mail: rainbowsolidarity4cuban5@gmail.com

For more information about the case of the Cuban Five, visit nyfreethefive.org or freethefive.org.

Barry Morley, secretary-treasurer of the Community Business and Professionals Association of Canada, states, *"It is time for the Bush administration to stop the hypocrisy and make terrorism against Cuba illegal."*

Chien San Feng, professor in the Department of Journalism, National Cheng Chi University, in Taipei, Taiwan, sends this message: *"The U.S. should lift the embargo."*

Dale Pfeiffer, author of "Eating Fossil Fuels," writes from Irvine, Ky.: *"It is long past time for the U.S. to recognize Cuba's right to determine its own form of government. In the years to come, U.S. respect for Cuba will be extremely important to the welfare of the U.S. public, as industrialized, U.S.-style agriculture results in a food crisis for which Cuba has pioneered the only possible solution. It is time to honor Cuba, not vilify it. Let this honor begin with the freedom of the Cuban Five."*

Adela, counselor at the Zig Zag Young Women's Resource Centre Inc. in Brisbane, Australia: *"As a citizen of the world, I demand the U.S. government to free the five Cubans who have not committed any crime. I also demand the U.S. government to lift the economic embargo against the Cuban people."*

Joan, from St. Paul, Minn.: *"I have written Fernando Gonzáles approximately twice a week since March of 2003. I have learned so much from him. The Five are examples for the world, just as the Cuban Revolution has always been an example for the world. I greatly appreciate your work in supporting the Five, and I know the Five and their families also greatly appreciate your beautiful efforts. Thank you!!!!!!"*

Melinda, a local co-founder of Code Pink in Willits, Calif., says of the Cuban Five: *"Thank you to all who have been fighting for their survival and publicity. They will be freed."*

Robert Taylor, from the Bus Riders Union/Labor Community Strategy Center, writes from Los Angeles, *"Let's keep the fight on to free the Cuban Five from jail!"*

Monty, from Jamul, Calif., stresses, *"Please get the word out to keep up the pressure."*

David, from New State, concludes: *"To all justice-loving people in the U.S. and around the world, we appeal to you to join the struggle to free Fernando, René, Antonio, Ramón and Gerardo. Help us in outreach, education and organizing, because once people know the facts of the case, we are sure they will call for their freedom as well."*

Cuba surpasses world on same-sex, trans rights

The Communist Party of Cuba has welcomed an update of the revolutionary Family Code to include same-sex and trans rights, reported National Center for Sexual Education (CENESEX) Director Mariela Castro Espín at the 5th International Culture and Development Congress held in Havana on June 11-14, 2007.

Journalist Dalia Costa reported from Havana on June 18, "If the initiative is approved, gay and lesbian couples would enjoy the same civil, patrimonial, inheritance, housing and adoption rights as heterosexual couples." (caribbean360.com)

Costa added, "Norma Guillart, an expert involved in the work of a group of lesbians in CENESEX, told IPS that the reform would also recognize the right of any woman to assisted reproduction services, which are currently limited to married couples."

Castro Espín said that in expectation of the legal changes, a request has already been filed with the Ministry of Public Health to provide reproductive assistance to three lesbian couples. (Cuban News Agency)

The amendment to the Family Code, Costa stated, would also "stipulate that the family has the responsibility and duty to accept and care for all of its members, regardless of their gender identity or sexual orientation."

The planned reform, drafted by the Federation of Cuban Women (FMC) and backed by CENESEX, will be introduced to the people's parliament as a draft law.

Same-sex marriage

Currently in the U.S., efforts by Republicans and Democrats—both political parties of capitalist big business—have pushed for reactionary legislation defining marriage as "between a man and a woman" solely to block the rights of same-sex couples.

But in Cuba, Article 36 of the Family Code of the revolutionary workers' state was defending the rights of women emerging from colonial and imperialist patriarchal enslavement when it codified in 1975 that "marriage is the voluntary union between a man and a woman."

In Cuba today, common law couples enjoy the same rights as married couples. And children all have the same rights, whether born to single women, couples who are unmarried, married, living together, separated or divorced. (caribbean360.com)

Ricardo Alarcón, president of Cuba's National Assembly, stated in the spring, "We have to abolish any form of discrimination" against homosexuality. He explained, "We

G.Dunkel

Activists brought Rainbow Solidarity for the Cuban Five and defense of the Cuban Revolution to Pride 2007 events in N.Y., L.A., Boston, Atlanta, Buffalo, San Diego and other cities. Above, Rainbow Solidarity signers Bev Hiestand (left) and Imani Henry (center).

are trying to see how to do that, whether it should be to grant them the right to marry or to have same-sex unions. We have to redefine the concept of marriage. Socialism should be a society that does not exclude anybody."

Castro Espín said that the proposal to add same-sex marriage to the Cuban Constitution will be taken up when that charter is next amended. "For now," she added, "it is sufficient to reform the Family Code, which is recognized as a branch of Cuban law."

In her presentation on the last day of the international congress, Castro Espín emphasized, "The political will exists to eliminate all forms of discrimination in our laws."

"Laws by themselves are not sufficient for achieving real change," she noted, but they are necessary to achieve forward momentum.

Trans rights moving forward

The proposed reforms to the Family Code also serve to bolster CENESEX's 2004 national strategy to support the needs of transsexual and transgender Cubans. This plan, Castro Espín explained, "is already being put into effect." (caribbean360.com)

The plan involves winning greater acceptance in the educational system and consciousness-raising among the revolutionary security forces.

Sex reassignment surgery—cost-free, like all forms of health care in Cuba—will be more available on request.

Twenty-four transsexual Cubans, who have won support from CENESEX since 1979, have applied for surgery. Many of them have already had their identity documents amended. Some 40 other Cubans have applied for sex-reassignment.

"Nearly everything is ready," Castro Espín concluded. "An internal Public Health Ministry regulation has authorized the performance of this surgery by the specialized health services, and work has been carried out in training staff and acquiring technology, medical supplies and prosthetics." ▼

BIBLIOGRAPHY

Cuban strategy in the struggle against AIDS. *Granma*, September 18, 1988.

Spotlight on Cuba's strategy against HIV/AIDS. 2001. *MEDICC review* II (1,2).

World Sexology Congress in Havana: Treading the path of human development. 2003. *Granma International*, March 19.

Cuban parliamentary committees conclude 2005 review. *Granma*, December, 2005

Cuban soap opera with gay story lines draws to an end; some see show as increased acceptance. *Advocate.com/Miami Herald* 2006 [cited November 8. Available from http://216.239.51.104/search?q=cache:AHKe5lKjbx0J:www.globalgayz.com/cuba-news03-06.html+Advocate+%22Now,+as+the+show+draws+to+an+end,:%22&hl=en&ct=clnk&cd=1&gl=us&client=firefox-a.

Cuban parliament to discuss free sex-changes. *Diversity (Diversidad)*, February 13, 2007.

Acosta, Dalia. A long-closed door opens for sexual diversity in Cuba. Inter Press Service (IPS) News Agency. 2004 [cited July 3. Available from http://mostlywater.org/rights_cuba_door_opens_for_sexual_diversity.

Aguilera, Elizabeth. AIDS: Cuba's low HIV rate belies the stigma, ignorance many face. *Denver Post*, February 10, 2003.

Arreola, Gerardo. Cuba divided on the issue of bisexuality. *La Jornada*, May 8, 2006.

———. Plans to authorize sex change operations and modifications in identity documents: Cuban Parliament considers legal recognition of the rights of transsexuals; Total endorsement from two commissions, says main promoter Mariela Castro. *La Jornada*, Jan. 9, 2006.

Bejel, Emilio. 2001. *Gay Cuban Nation*. Chicago: The University of Chicago Press

Berkowitz, Bill. Viva gay Cuba! Out and married in the increasingly tolerant Communist island. Workingforchange.com 2001 [cited July 13. Available from http://www.workingforchange.com/article.cfm?ItemID=11550.

Betancourt, José Luis Estrada. 2006. Unseen faces (The hidden side of the moon). *Juventud Rebelde*, newspaper of the Unión de Jóvenes Comunistas (Union of Young Communists).

Bjorklund, Eva. 2000. Homosexuality is not illegal in Cuba, but like elsewhere, homophobia persists. *Swedish Cuba* magazine quarterly, published by the Swedish-Cuban Association, Summer.

Borge, Tomas. 1992. *Face to Face with Fidel Castro: A Conversation with Tomás Borge:* Ocean Press.

Buchanan, Patrick. AIDS disease: it's nature striking back. *New York Post*, May 24, 1983.

Burton, Richard. 1886. *The Book of the Thousand Nights and a Night*, Vol. I.

Cabral, Juan Pérez. Gays wed in Cuba: the second revolution. theGully.com 2001 [cited June 21. Available from http://216.239.51.104/search?q=cache:ofJMmdKcg2IJ:www.thegully.com/essays/cuba/010621gay_cuba.html+Cabral+Gays+wed+in+Cuba%3F&hl=en&ct=clnk&cd=1&gl=us&client=firefox-a.

Cardenal, Ernesto. 1974. *In Cuba*. New York: New Directions Publishing Corporation.

Cookson, Clive. Cuba praised for its AIDS programme. *Financial Times*, February 16, 2003.

Eaton, Tracey. Sex conference in Cuba covers everything from implants to abuse. *The Dallas Morning News*, April 1, 2003.

Editors. 2001. Cuba's HIV-AIDS rate: Lowest in the Americas. *MEDICC review* II (1,2).

———. 2001. Cuba's strategy against HIV/AIDS. *MEDICC review* II (1,2).

Fee, Elizabeth. 1988. Sex education in Cuba: An interview with Dr. Celestino Alvarez Lajonchere. *International Journal of Health Services* 18 (2).

Feinberg, Leslie. 1996. *Transgender Warriors: Making History from Joan of Arc to Ru Paul*. Hardcover ed. Boston: Beacon Press.

———. Bobbi Campbell calls for solidarity in fight against AIDS. *Workers World*, October 13, 1983

———. Demonstrators in 7 cities demand gov't funds to fight AIDS. *Workers World*, 1983..

———. 'The government didn't care if I lived or died': Workers World interviews Michael Callen who has AIDS. *Workers World*, August 25, 1983.

Fuente, Alejandro de la. 2004. Slave law and claims-making in Cuba: The Tannenbaum debate revisited. *Law and History Review* 22 (2).

Garcia, Eduardo Jimenez. Gay rights in Cuba: How much has changed? *Green Left Weekly*.

Gilpin, Margaret and Luis Felipe Bernaza. 1995. Mariposas en el Andamio (Butterflies on the Scaffold).

González, Fernán. Mariela Castro: 'I am proud of my father.' *BBC Mundo*, September 18, 2006.

Green, Richard. 1974. Historical and Cross-Cultural Survey. In *Sexual Identity Conflict in Children and Adults*, New York: Basic Books.

Guerra, Francisco. 1971. *The Pre-Columbian Mind*. London: Seminar Press.

Hatch, Marcel and Leonardo Hechavarría. 2001. Gays in Cuba, from the Hollywood school of falsification. Review of reviewed item. (October), http://www.walterlippmann.com/lgbt-cuba-003.html.

Hillson, Jon. 2001. The Sexual Politics of Reinaldo Arenas: Fact, Fiction and the Real Record of the Cuban Revolution.

Israel, Esteban. Castro's niece fights for new revolution. *Reuters*, July 3, 2006.

Iznaga, Diana. 1986. Introduction in *Los negros curros*, by Fernando Ortiz. Havana: Editorial de Ciencias Sociales.

Lafitau, Joseph François. 1724. *Moeurs des sauvages ameriquains, compares aux moeurs des premiers temps*. 2 vols. Vol. 1:52 Paris: Saugrain.

Lamey, Mary. Mariela Castro speaks out for Cuba's gay minority. *The Gazette*, July 29, 2006.

Levin, Julia. 2003. Tomás Gutiérrez Alea. *Senses of cinema*.

López, Marlon Brito. *Art and Love vs. AIDS: Part 1*. 2006 [cited. Available from http://216.239.51.104/search?q=cache:NQ3tPk4Q4r8J:www.walterlippmann.com/docs669.html+Marlon+ Brito+Lopez+%22The+main+goals%22&hl=en&ct=clnk&cd=1&gl=us&client=firefox-a.

Lumsden, Ian. 1996. *Machos, Maricones, and Gays*. Philadelphia: Temple University Press.

Magalhães, Pedro de. 1922. *The Histories of Brazil*. New York: The Cortes Society.

Manago, Cleo. 1994. *Cuba, from a Black, Male, Same-Gender-Loving Perspective.* Sonoma County Free Press, August.

Marcy, Sam. The U.S.-Cuba immigration accord. *Workers World,* September 22, 1994.

Marquette, Jacques. 1896-1901. *Of the First Voyage Made by Father Marquette Toward New Mexico, and How the Idea Thereof Was Conceived.* Edited by R. G. Thwaites. Vol. 59, *The Jesuit and Allied Documents.* Cleveland: Burrows.

Marx, Gary. Helping Cubans realize 'what it means to be gay', June 4, 2006.

Marx, Karl. 1970. *The German Ideology,* New York: International Publishers.

McCubbin, Bob. Gay Cuba: Problems of building socialism. *Workers World,* April 26, 2001.

McKinley, James C. Jr. Cuba counters prostitution with AIDS programs. *New York Times,* December 26, 2004.

Mejía, Max. 2000. Mexican Pink. In *Different Rainbows,* edited by P. Drucker: Gay Men's Press.

Mutti, Joseph. *'Repression' Saved Lives.* Resource Center of the Americas.org 1999 [cited. Available from http://www.americas.org/item_260.

Oberg, Larry R. 2006. The status of gays in Cuba: myth and reality. *Cuban Libraries Solidarity Group.*

Pratt, Minnie Bruce. 'Gay Cuba': Revolution within the revolution. *Workers World,* July 12, 2001.

Puyol, Johanna. Interview with Rafael Cheíto González: An open message. *La Jiribilla,* April 28, 2006.

Ramonet, Ignacio. 2006. *Cien Horas Con Fidel.* Translated by e. b. W. L. CubaNews translation: Cuban Council of State.

Reed, Gail A. 2006. MR Interview: Mariela Castro, MS—Director, National Center for Sex Education. *MEDICC review* VIII (No. 1).

Rich, B. Ruby and Lourdes Arguelles.1989. Homosexuality, homophobia, and revolution: notes toward an understanding of the Cuban lesbian and gay male experience. In *Hidden from History: Reclaiming the Gay & Lesbian Past,* edited by M. V. a. G. C. Martin Bauml Duberman, Jr. New York: New American Library. Original edition, *Signs, A Journal of Women in Culture and Society,* Summer 1984.

Rodriguez, Andrea. Cuba's transsexuals get powerful new friend. Associated Press, September 5, 2004. [cited Sept. 5. Available from http://www.ap.org.

Vries, Sonja de. *Gay Cuba:* Frameline Distribution.

———. N. California queers help celebrate: a gay May Day in Havana. *News for a Peoples World,* May 26, 1995.

Wald, Karen. Health official details drastic approach to AIDS. *Guardian,* October 28, 1987.

West, Dennis. 1995. 'Strawberry and Chocolate,' ice cream and tolerance: Interview with Tomás Gutiérrez Alea. *Cineaste* 21 (1-2):16-20.

Williams, Walter. 1986. *The Spirit and the Flesh: Sexual Diversity in American Indian Culture.* Boston: Beacon Press.

Wills, Stephen J. and Randolph E. Risch. Positive views of gays. *Gay Insurgent,* Summer, 1980.

Feinberg, hoisting flag aloft, at Buffalo, N.Y., Youth Against War & Fascism (YAWF) protest against 1973 CIA-engineered counter-revolution in Chile.

ABOUT THE AUTHOR

Leslie Feinberg is a long-time activist and award-winning author of the novels *Stone Butch Blues* and *Drag King Dreams*, and the non-fiction works *Transgender Warriors: Making History from Joan of Arc to Dennis Rodman*, and *Trans Liberation: Beyond Pink or Blue*. Feinberg's web-book-in-progress—*Lavender & Red*—can be read online at: www.workers.org.

Feinberg is in the national leadership of Workers World Party; a managing editor of *Workers World* newspaper; member of the LGBT Caucus of the National Writers Union/UAW; Pride At Work, AFL-CIO; and associate member of the Steelworkers Union. Feinberg is also a founder of Rainbow Flags for Mumia and a national organizer for the International Action Center. Feinberg is an initiator of Rainbow Solidarity for the Cuban Five and takes the demand to free the Five, and defense of the Cuban Revolution, to campuses, rallies, community events and youth groups across the U.S. and internationally. For more information about the Rainbow Solidarity call, look for the rainbow at: www.nyfreethefive.org.

Leslie Feinberg is at home in cyberspace at www.transgenderwarrior.org and can be emailed at leslie@workers.org.

Lavender & Red

by Leslie Feinberg

This book in progress, written in weekly installments in *Workers World* newspaper, explores the relationship over more than a century between the liberation of oppressed sexualities, genders and sexes, and the communist movement. You can read the entire, ongoing series online at:

www.workers.org/lavender-red/

INDEX